Praise for *Ethnic Flames of the Burning Bush*

"This is an important book that will help all congregations to do justice both to our shared identity in Christ and to our cultural distinctives. Tokerau Joseph provides us with the theological reflection and the direction we need to resist the powerful pull towards homogeneity in our life together."

Dr Tim Cooper,
Professor of Church History, University of Otago

"All around the world people are on the move in what has been called the new migration. Largely this is from majority world countries to the west, creating significant ethnic diversity where there was previously a significant European majority, and New Zealand is at the leading edge of this. Many of these people are Christian, and initially they established their own ethnic churches, but as they move into the second generation and beyond most desire to be in multiethnic churches, and research shows these are the most rapidly growing churches. Tokerau Joseph's work explores this in the context of Aotearoa New Zealand and provides a highly needed understanding, some helpful practical insights, and a solid theological base to help churches engage with this challenging but much needed task."

Rev Dr Kevin Ward, former Senior Lecturer and
Acting Principal of Knox Centre for Ministry and Leadership

"This is a significant book. For far too long the Pacific presence in New Zealand and its churches has been siloed, hidden from view in strong but isolated Pasifika churches in very specific churches. But now a very significant moment is happening gradually as Pasifika people mostly from the generation born in this country sit down beside us, their Palagi brothers and sisters. It is a development that cannot be taken for granted and must involve changes for all of us. Tokerau Joseph has researched the issue and now brings us the book we need. I urge all to read this book carefully and digest its implications carefully. And I thank its author for boldly pioneering the way."

Dr Peter Lineham,
Professor Emeritus of History, Massey University

"A superb piece of practical and public theology arising from generous cultural insight, solid sociological and theological research, and the wisdom born of personal involvement.

Dr Joseph displays a deeply committed curiosity about how communities seeking to embody Christian ideals of unity with the welcoming affirmation of human diversity live out the practical challenges of life together.

His timely work is of relevance for politics as well as for our churches in general and the well-being of the country."

Rev Dr John Roxburgh,
Honorary Fellow, Theology Programme, University of Otago

Ethnic Flames of the Burning Bush

An Exploration of Ethnic Relations in Congregations of the Presbyterian Church of Aotearoa New Zealand

Tokerau Joseph

Philip
Garside
Publishing Ltd.

Email Tokerau at: tokerau.j@gmail.com

Paperback International edition 2024:
ISBN 9781991027610

Also available
New Zealand paperback: ISBN 9781991027603
Paperback print-on-demand USA: ISBN 9798864823170

PDF: ISBN 9781991027627
ePub/Kindle/Mobi: ISBN 9781991027634

Philip Garside Publishing Ltd
PO Box 17160
Wellington 6147
New Zealand
books@pgpl.co.nz – www.philipgarsidebooks.com

Cover image:
Adapted from PCANZ official logo

Contents

Dedication

All praise and glory to God for making this book possible.

I honour my wife Tangi, our children, and grandchildren,
for their constant support and sacrifice to bring this task to
life. Gratitude is also due to our wider family and Cook Islands
community for your affirmation over the years.

Thank you for sharing my passion and pain.
Your encouraging words have been a source of strength
for me to persevere.

I dedicate this work to you, Tangi
and the late papa Enoka Taana.

Kia akameitakiia te Atua.

Introduction

For some people, cross-cultural experiences can be meaningful and enriching; for others they can be distressing and painful. People can either continue to work through ethnically and culturally diverse relations or they can retreat into ones that reflect familiarity and homogeneity. The former may be what people aspire to have, but the latter is perhaps the reality and easier option requiring less effort to get along with others. Church congregations face exactly this challenge.

Imagine an ethnically diverse congregation comprising mainly of two ethnic groups – European and Pacific Islander. The latter consists of two island nationalities from the South Pacific: Samoan and Cook Islander. There are also very small numbers of people of Asian descent who usually fellowship with the European members. By and large, the three groups have separate weekly worship services conducted in their respective languages at different times on a Sunday. In more recent years, they have all worshipped together in one service to celebrate Holy Communion. In these combined worship services their languages are incorporated through prayers, scripture readings, hymns, and within the Communion liturgy. It is a multi-lingual worship service which is printed on a service sheet. When the Samoan or Cook Islands language is used, translation into English is provided. This, however, is not reciprocated for Samoans and Cook Islanders when English is used. Sometimes the language of other ethnic minority groups (Mandarin, Hungarian or Tokelauan) is used, but with an English translation. Attempts are made to have a reasonably balanced content of languages in the service, though overall English is used more often than the other languages, to the advantage of European members who have been part of the congregation the longest.

But there is disquiet about their relationship. Some European parishioners say that the combined Communion service should be conducted only in English because they cannot understand or pronounce non-English words that are foreign to them. They validate this stance with the understanding that ever since the early European settlers established the congregation, Holy Communion had always been conducted in English. As the Samoans and Cook Islanders were later arrivals into the congregation, they should follow the pattern already established, rather than the other way round. By incorporating the other non-English languages, the European parishioners feel as if the worship service they were accustomed to is being taken away from them, thus leaving them without a real sense of connection within the worship service. They say that they have no problem fellowshipping together in worship with those who are ethnically and culturally different from them, as long as the majority of the worship content is done in English. To keep everyone happy and to make Holy Communion more meaningful, it was suggested that each group of the congregation should revert to celebrating Holy Communion in its own respective language and worship service.

The above scenario is unsettling for me. It brings a sense of unease because it reflects some of the honest struggles and pain of congregations I have served during my ministry journey as a parish minister. This case above is drawn from experiences in my ministry at First Church of Otago, but it is also gleaned from some of the relationship dynamics during my time in a pan-Pacific congregation, Otara Pacific Islanders' Presbyterian Church in South Auckland. In this congregation, relations were clearly drawn along ethnic/cultural lines between island groups and the clergy ministry team. We tried hard to make joint activities work, and I think most people genuinely perceived our unity as a positive thing, but the effort required to maintain our cooperative endeavours was also testing. Although not spoken about openly by parishioners, most demonstrated their religiosity by committing more often to their own ethno-cultural setting.

I present these situations not to convey a negative portrayal of my congregations or ministry, but to highlight some of the challenges and realities of ethnic relations within Christian communities. In both congregations, people were trying to work out how best to exercise their Christian faith in light of their culturally diverse life together. We were and still are learning how to live together in unity and diversity; individuals and different groups negotiating ways to affirm both their cultural and religious identities. They could easily do this on their own; the real challenge is how they can do it together.

This book is based on my doctoral thesis that explored how ethnic relations shape local congregations of the Presbyterian Church of Aotearoa New Zealand (PCANZ). Although I will not present data as fully as in a thesis, what I do offer is nonetheless an exercise in practical theology arising out of my reflection on the questions we wrestle with in the praxis of life and ministry.

The circumstances from First Church raise deeper questions. How should an ethnically diverse congregation organise itself so that it is faithful to what it believes to be the church? In order to save a diverse community from cultural tensions when worshipping together, would it be better for ethnic groups to worship separately? Would it be more culturally appropriate to function separately from other Christian brothers and sisters who are different? The end result might be that, instead of being one congregation consisting of three ethnic groups, they eventually become separate churches. If that happens, what does that say about what it means to be the church of Jesus Christ?

The overt issue in the situation described above is about language, but beneath that is a more fundamental issue: Christian identity and fellowship together as church. It raises the subject of ecclesiology, the doctrine or theology of the Church. What does it mean to be the Church or, as Alister McGrath pertinently asks, "What sort of body is the church?"[1] Other questions arise. Is it theologically acceptable for Christian congregations to be ethnically homogeneous in composition? Is it theologically acceptable for the ministry of congregations to be organised along ethnic and cultural lines? What informs the practices of congregations? Is it their ecclesiology or is it the ethnic and cultural preferences of their members?

These questions may not be easy to answer, but they are important. I address them with a focus primarily upon ethnic relations within my own denomination of the PCANZ. In particular, I examine this with respect to its four main ethnic groups – European, Māori, Asian and Pacific Islander. By 'European' I mean those, including descendants of earlier immigrants to New Zealand, who primarily identify themselves with a Caucasian heritage of Western/ European origins. 'Māori' are those who consider their chief identity as Māori or indigenous people (*tangata whenua* – people of the land) of New Zealand. Like 'European', the terms 'Asian' and 'Pacific Islander' are applied to those of Asian or Pacific Islander heritage and who primarily uphold this identity for themselves in New Zealand. I acknowledge that these could be construed as restrictive identity terms that some people do not choose or accept for themselves. They have been chosen to describe the general area of origin for people groups such as Europe, Asia, and the islands of the South Pacific. The ethnic identity of particular groups (for example, Cook Islanders and Niueans within the generic term Pacific Islanders; or Koreans and Chinese under the umbrella of Asians) are valid in their own right and will be used to make clear distinctions between specific groups.

Perhaps it is pertinent to clarify some things at this point. Terms such as ethnicity, race, and nationality are fluid.[2] They are essentially "social constructions, the product of specific historical and geographical forces, rather than biologically given ideas whose meaning is dictated by nature."[3]

Ethnicity is viewed not so much as an isolated entity but as the result of the constant encounters between different peoples. According to Michael Fischer, ethnicity is something that is "reinvented and reinterpreted in each generation."[4] Ethnic identity is thus malleable; individuals negotiate racial and nationalist attributions amidst a variety of social constraints. As people of a particular ethnic group move from one place to another, obviously they face new sets of social constraints, and negotiate over time how their identity is lived out for them in their new context. For example, a New Zealand-born Cook Islander may embrace an ethnicity that incorporates two nationalities and cultural identities. Therefore, "ethnicity" and "culture" can often be used interchangeably to mean the same thing.

My focus here is on the relations of these four generic ethnic groups within the PCANZ at various levels, but with particular attention to the congregation level. They are part of a bigger story within the PCANZ that clearly involves issues of ethnicity, culture, identity and belonging. This includes my story, in which others have often commented to me about Pacific Islanders in general and Cook Islanders specifically as "your people." This is despite the fact that I am of both Cook Islands and European (Scottish and English) heritage, although I look more European than Cook Islander. I am fluent in both Cook Islands Māori language and English, and very comfortable in the company of people ethnically different from me. Such words seem to suggest that I am not part of those who say them to me; that I do not belong with them or them with me, or we together. Yet I feel connected to them.

As in my own ministry experiences, people are trying to find ways to co-exist religiously and culturally in their faith community. They are challenged to gain a new self-understanding in relation to others who are different from them. At the same time, they are also encouraged to know others so that together they might better appreciate and live out the larger identity they share as Christians, as the church of Jesus Christ. Exploring these issues may not be comfortable because they may identify blind-spots of prejudice, bias or discriminatory attitudes and practices within groups and individuals that trigger conflict. However, acknowledging such tensions is at least a beginning point for working through them so that we might eventually live out more faithfully our life together as people of God. This requires grappling with our cultural preferences and our theological understanding of what it means to be the church.

This reality gives rise to the title of this book: "Ethnic Flames of the Burning Bush." The emblem of the PCANZ depicts the burning bush from Exodus 3:1-2, where "the bush was blazing, yet it was not consumed." Being ablaze, the bush is expected to burn itself out. Yet, beyond expectation, it remains intact and is not consumed. This is a mystery, and so is the way that ethnic flames are burning at the local congregational level of the PCANZ. Just as God spoke to Moses through the burning bush about hope and liberation for God's people from a restrictive life in Egypt, I hope that we may discern together what God might also be saying to you and other Christian communities about the kind of church we are called to be.

In chapter one, we examine literature of research done on how ethnic relations have shaped religious communities overseas and within the New Zealand context. Chapter two explores a Christological and Trinitarian ecclesiology to gain theological perspectives of how ethnic relations 'fit' within church life. Then we will look at how those views are exercised within the structures and processes of the PCANZ at global, national and regional levels. To appreciate the reality of PCANZ congregations today, chapter three will review the development of Presbyterianism among the four main ethnic groupings to identify how these people groups became agents of their respective cultural hopes. In chapter four we will examine the reality of ethnic relations at the congregational level. It will reveal just how ethnically homogeneous or diverse congregations are and the extent to which ethnic relations shape the practices of parishioners and clergy. Finally, I offer some thoughts as both a challenge and encouragement to people in congregations about how they can live out more faithfully our ecclesiology of unity in diversity. These include re-evaluating our Christian identity, cross-cultural engagements, a pan-Pacific model of church, and the sacrament of Holy Communion.

I strongly suspect that all kinds of church congregations are shaped by the ethnic relations of peoples within them. Although my focus of this is within my own Presbyterian tradition, the hope is that, as you continue to read, you might reflect upon and discover insights from your own religio-ethnic experiences in the faith community to which you belong.

1 — Ethnicity Matters

In recent decades there has been growing interest in research about how religious groups organise themselves. Particular attention has been drawn to how ethnicity might influence the dynamic of such groups. Examining literature from various fields of sociological research may help us answer the basic question of whether or not ethnic and cultural relations matter between people. If they do, then such analysis will shed light on how people order their religious life together. Exploring different contexts may reveal whether people generally prefer engaging in ways that affirm ethnic similarity or diversity. These contexts include religious communities within the United States and New Zealand. Not only may they assist in our efforts to understand the extent to which ethnicity matters to people, they may also reveal how it might shape the communities to which they belong. Our exploration may also provide indicators for a similar dynamic in congregations of the PCANZ.

Religious Communities Overseas

Within the last few decades disciplines such as sociology have given more consideration to the relationship between the ethnicity or race of people and their religiosity. Much of this research has focused on religious communities in the United States. Despite the population of the United States becoming increasingly ethnically and culturally diverse, its churches remain largely ethnic-specific.[5] Utilising data from the National Congregations Study by sociologist Mark Chaves, Emerson and Kim calculate that nearly nine out of every ten American congregations consist of at least 90% of one ethnic group, while 80% of congregations are represented by 95% of a particular ethnic group.[6] To identify a congregation as ethnically diverse, they applied a formula in which no one ethnic group comprises 80% or more of the total congregation. From this they conclude that just over seven percent of their congregation sample was ethnically diverse.[7] Although racial integration has been occurring in other institutions in the United States, the vast majority of the more than 300,000 congregations consist of members who are of the same race.[8]

Although such research has shown that the church is one of the most homogeneous of American institutions, there are variations. Kevin Dougherty has found that patterns of diversity differ by faith group, region and location size. For example, Protestant churches tend to be more ethnic-specific, whereas Catholic churches are inclined to be more diverse; churches in the American West tend to be more ethnically diverse than in other regions; and churches in urban areas are more likely to be heterogeneous compared to churches in rural areas, which are usually homogeneous.[9]

Dougherty also found that socio-economic similarities between people did not necessarily give rise to ethnically diverse communities so much as the region in which such communities were located and the faith group or tradition to which they were attached.[10] In other words, geographic location and the type of church or tradition to which people belong tend to reflect ethnic preferences more than other factors.

Within a particular geographical area, people may also go to some lengths to be part of their religious community. Sinha, Hillier, Cnaan and McGrew examine congregations and the commuting trends of their members in the city of Philadelphia. They find that all but five of the 1,340 churches in their sample had 75% or more members of the same ethnicity, and their data confirms that people are willing to commute longer distances to worship with "co-ethnics."[11] They also identify that despite the socio-economic differences between Whites, Blacks, Asians and Hispanics, people who share the same ethnicity, language, traditions and customs tend to congregate together even when they do not live in the same area.[12]

This suggests that although the population of communities may be ethnically diverse, people from such communities are still prepared to cross geographic boundaries to attend churches that specifically affirm their religious and ethnic identity. This finding goes beyond the understanding that ethnic-specific churches usually reflect the population in which they are located.[13]

The larger research question may be put this way: Why are most religious communities in America ethnically homogeneous? George Yancey believes the history of racism and discrimination in America is a significant part of the answer. The development of ethnocentrism creates barriers that alienate people from each other. "These divisions are based upon real racial problems that exist in our society and have germinated over a long period of time. Only after we realize the extent of the racial strife that exists in the United States, and realize that this strife will not easily disappear, can we appreciate the difficulty of developing multiracial congregations."[14]

Another part of the answer may relate to social and religious pluralism and the way American religion is organised: people increasingly have a choice in the "religious marketplace" to belong with others like themselves.[15] Relating the work of Lois Verbrugge on adult friendships to the church context, Emerson and Smith also found that "social associations between like people are more stable. And stability enables the creation of meaning and belonging, the very reasons people seek and need social associations and groups ... So the attraction to people of similar persons and groups has much to do with fulfilling basic human needs."[16] This highlights the point that, although people want to congregate together to fulfil their basic human need of belonging, they tend to do so in ethnic-specific ways that affirm a particular identity. Other reasons for the appeals of such settings are that people usually feel socially comfortable with others like them. This shields them from the negative forces of racism and cultural tensions or differences; in addition, most people have had more experience in homogeneous contexts than in diverse ones.[17]

Groups who form unique identities for themselves, whether based on ethnicity, socio-economic or some other status, are sometimes called "niches." C. Peter Wagner sees "niche churches" as being beneficial in terms of growth. The reception and development of Christian faith is grounded in the idea that people "should be encouraged to become Christians right where they are" within their ethnic and cultural context.[18] Since people generally prefer to associate with others ethnically similar to themselves, without the tensions of cultural differences, such groups are believed to have a better chance at growing numerically.[19]

This view supports Donald McGavran's "Homogeneous Unit Principle," which argues that each ethnic entity (tribe, nation, people group) should have an opportunity to have the Christian message and community developed in their own cultural context. McGavran is perhaps best remembered for his assumption that people like to become Christians without having to cross cultural barriers: "It takes no great acumen to see that when marked differences of color, stature, income, cleanliness, and education are present, men [sic] understand the gospel better when expounded by their own kind of people. They prefer to join churches whose members look, talk, and act like themselves."[20] However, a growing critique of this view is that it seems to be theologically questionable.[21] The fact that Christians may feel more comfortable with others with whom they are ethnically and culturally matched, and decide not to fellowship with other Christians who are different, can be seen as a form of ecclesiastical segregation.

Despite the appeal of ethnic and cultural familiarity, niche churches have not always translated into growth. George Yancey's own data indicates that, over a period of a year, ethnically diverse congregations rather than homogeneous ones were more likely to experience growth.[22] So there is no clear evidence that homogeneous congregations grow faster than diverse ones; in any case, the latter are still obviously very much a minority.

While ethnically homogeneous churches may affirm group identity and solidarity, differences between people may be the reason why ethnically diverse churches are rare. This is the view of scholars who propose that racial integration in religious organisations requires a much higher cost to achieve.[23] For example, Emerson and Christerson identify that there can be costs to both groups and individuals in ethnically diverse congregations. If they do not feel integrated into the life of the congregation, and if their worth or concerns are ignored or devalued by others different from them, they can feel pushed to the edges of congregational life and they lose something of their religio-ethnic identity, compared to what they could receive in an ethnically homogeneous congregation.[24] Ethnically mixed churches have to work harder to achieve solidarity and unity by focusing on developing a common culture rather than on ethnic identity. In ethnically diverse churches, developing a common life together is very important, but extremely challenging because of ethnic and cultural differences between people groups.

In her study of 23 congregations in the United States, Nancy Ammerman discovered that the value of a shared church culture with an inclusive organisational identity could overcome the limitations rooted in ethnic differences.[25] However, she concedes that a shared congregational life can happen only to the extent that diverse cultural practices of members are first acknowledged and accepted by others in the congregation.[26] For this reason, congregations represented by a mix of ethnicities have to be more understanding, patient and accepting of each other to make their diverse relationships work. The scenario regarding First Church testifies to these findings.

The leadership in ethnically diverse churches can play an important role in how ethnic relations might work out in congregations. Charles Foster argues that a "transformative, anticipatory and relational" approach is helpful to the ethnic and cultural dynamic.[27] By this he means that church leaders, particularly clergy, must look beyond the ethnic focus, although not excluding it, and pay careful attention to collective practices that nurture healthy change, promote a shared vision or hope, and build caring relationships in diverse groups.[28]

These sentiments are echoed by sociologist and church minister Gerardo Marti, who reflects on the dynamic in his own church, called "Mosaic."[29] Although Marti asserts that his church is multi-ethnic, it does not emphasise the expression of one's Christian faith through ethnic or cultural practices. Instead, his ministry incorporates the contemporary popular culture of its society in an attempt to accommodate those already assimilated into it and who value their Christian identity over and above their ethnic identity: "Mosaic is a place where ethnicity is more often obscured, making way for a shared religious identity. The strategic management of a constructed and negotiated religious identity is the central work of charismatic authority within this multiethnic congregation. While the people of Mosaic embrace a religious label, they consistently avoid ethnic labels."[30]

Ethnically diverse churches like Mosaic tend to focus more on a "Christian" identity expressed through practices that are perceived to be "neutral" to all its members. One might ask, however, whether this view at Mosaic is an attempt to be colour-blind and culture-bland, as if the ethnic elements of its members could not contribute to and enhance the common faith they express. Being colour-blind and working only with a Christian identity is perhaps easier than seeing the various cultural distinctions and having to cater appropriately to their particular needs. As earlier observed, an approach like this would require more effort to maintain. A further challenge would be the degree to which members want to promote the particular cultural expression of their faith that might encourage ethnic enclaves, as opposed to a "neutral" or Christian identity that seeks diversity in fellowship. The development of ethnic enclaves may also create a sense of distance between Christians.

Splitting ethnic identity from cultural practice is not easy. They are in many ways intertwined. Everyday challenges of racism, ethnocentrism or lack of cultural competence can limit the degree to which diverse peoples can meaningfully engage in religious settings. In looking at the city of Las Vegas, Nevada, Damon Hodge showed that it was more challenging, though not impossible, for clergy to work cross-culturally: "A black preacher may not be able to reach some rich white kid in the suburbs ... white preachers also may be unable to connect with black believers."[31]

What Hodge observed indicates that the effectiveness of the clergy/congregation relationship may have more to do with ethnic connections than purely religious ones (doctrinal or theological). In other words, ethnicity matters in religious life. Yet our ecclesiology asserts that Christian identity, and not ethnicity, is the primary basis of belonging together in the church and that it is an identity which transcends ethnic boundaries. Despite the difficulties of cross-cultural experiences between Christians who are ethnically different, there is theological support for it.

Is there a correlation between the ethnicity of a congregation and that of clergy? This is a question that has been relatively unexplored by researchers. For one predominantly White church it was observed that, as African-American and Latino clergy were successively appointed, African-American and Latino locals began attending.[32] However, due to the tensions with the long-time White members of the congregation brought about by these changes, which included differing styles of worship, the African-Americans and Hispanics eventually left to join congregations that consisted largely of people who were ethnically and culturally similar to them.

Work by Neal Krause on the self-esteem of older people in regard to their engagement with clergy sheds some light on the relationship between clergy and congregation members.[33] In studying the self-esteem in Black and White individuals based upon their interactions with clergy, he found that because of the perceived central role of clergy and church in the Black community, the emotional support from clergy tends to bolster the self-esteem of older Blacks, more so than is the case with older Whites. The results further indicated that negative interaction with clergy is associated with diminished feelings of self-worth, but no significant difference was noted in this regard between Blacks or Whites.[34]

Despite the usefulness of Krause's work, it does not make explicit the ethnicity of clergy in relation to those in the study sample. Instead, it leads one to presume that Blacks and Whites in his sample belonged to largely homogeneous communities that had Black and White clergy respectively. Therefore, regardless of the quality of the relationship between clergy and community members, they seem to occur within ethnically similar contexts, further indicating the significance of ethnicity in such settings. It would be interesting to clearly identify whether there is a correlation between the ethnicity of clergy and that of the predominant group of congregations.

To grasp a better understanding of the ethnic relationship between clergy and congregations, an examination of ethnic-specific first-generation immigrant churches may assist us. Such churches, as centres for cultural preservation as well as religious identity, provide a "religio-ethnic identity" that is integral for the settling of new immigrants into a new society and culture.[35] The cultural/social services that ethnic-specific immigrant congregations offer also reinforce home-land connections that include clergy with whom they are ethnically and culturally matched.[36]

Timothy Tseng's research has found that, although such clergy play a very central role in immigrant churches, the relationship with them is more generationally focused.[37] For Korean congregations in America, the leadership of immigrant churches requires people who are adept at observing Korean religious and cultural protocols. As bearers of Korean culture, home-land clergy in some ways resemble traditional religious roles such as that of a shaman or monk, and are therefore held in great respect, particularly by the older first-generation Koreans.[38]

However, second- and third-generation Asian Americans who have been assimilated into American society can find it increasingly difficult to relate with such clergy. For example, despite clergy being well versed in the language and customs from Korea, they are very limited in their ministry to the different generations of Americanised Koreans and usually ill-equipped to lead Asian-American congregations.[39] Regardless of how different generations relate with their ministers, they are relationships that continue to operate within an ethnic-specific setting.[40]

Similarly, studying second-generation Korean American students in university campus ministries, Rebecca Y. Kim observed that although these students participated in more inclusive and ethnically diverse settings, they still continued to draw ethnic boundaries for groups in which they were involved.[41] Using an interactive model of ethnic group and religious group formation, she identified three basic reasons why such students chose to revert to their own ethnic grouping.

First, they have more opportunity to participate in ethnic-specific organisations that interact within an ethnically dense and diverse structural setting. Second, they have a desire for what is most familiar because of the cultural ascriptions imposed upon them by American society at large. Third, they have a desire for power and majority-group status that interacts with continued racial marginalisation.[42] When second-generation American Koreans are outside their ethnic-specific context, the pull of cultural familiarity is still strong enough to keep them involved with Korean-American religious settings led by Koreans. Kim's work is helpful because it reflects much of what has already been examined: people prefer their own kind. If people, particularly minority groups, are inclined to gravitate toward their own ethnic-specific religious community, regardless of the opportunities to fellowship with others dissimilar to them, then parallel trends could be found for European, Māori, Asians and Pacific Islanders in the PCANZ.

Although much has already been said about ethnic-specific congregations, another dynamic, the pan-ethnic congregation, must also be considered. In America, pan-Asian congregations provide an opportunity for Asian Americans to move from a homogeneous context into one that may appear similar, yet diverse at the same time. Russell Jeung notes that although there are ethnic and cultural differences between Koreans, Chinese, Japanese and Vietnamese, for example, both congregation members and clergy of such groups who choose to discontinue their participation within their ethnic-specific churches still lean towards joining pan-Asian congregations.[43] The pan-Asian context appears to offer a more comfortable diversity as well as a shared new identity as "Asian-Americans," than being in non-Asian congregations.[44] This is not to say that Asian-Americans are not interested in multi-ethnic churches, but the reality of the ethnic diversity of such churches is still a challenge for pan-Asian congregations.

> New multiethnic churches have not been truly successful in becoming multiracial in membership. If a multiracial congregation is defined as a church where no one racial group is 80% or more of the membership, only two of the eight multiethnic congregations studied here may be considered truly multiethnic or multiracial. Although each of these churches has a strong mix of Chinese, Taiwanese, Korean, and Japanese, along with some other Asian groups represented, none has more than 30% of another racial group represented.[45]

It appears that, despite attempts to be more ethnically diverse, religious organisations still have a tendency to be homogeneous. Jeung's observation of pan-Asian congregations highlights that, although people may want to experience ethnic diversity in their religious settings, holding on to some form of homogeneity is nonetheless preferable for some.

Despite the challenges that an ethnically diverse or pan-ethnic congregation faces, the relationship with its leadership is one that may help shape the ethnic representation within it. George Yancey argues that having an ethnically diverse leadership can help facilitate a congregation's diversity because it can provide some assurances, particularly to minority groups, that they are represented and can have their concerns heard rather than become invisible and alienated.[46] As well as being able to attract different peoples to a congregation, ethnically diverse leadership may also play an important role in promoting an inclusive worship style.

Again, Yancey contends that incorporating and balancing the different ethnic cultures of a congregation in worship demonstrates an atmosphere of acceptance of one another and ensures that none of the ethnic groups "feels short-changed by the worship style."[47] These observations are useful because they show that ethnicity does matter in the relationship between congregation and clergy (or leadership). It matters because it has the potential to affirm either ethnic and cultural homogeneity or diversity of representation and practices in a congregation.

Exploring a sampling of religious contexts within the United States showed that ethnic relations do matter to people. This is reflected in the fact that most churches are ethnically homogeneous rather than diverse. There may be various reasons why people belong to such churches, but their preference for fellowshipping with others with whom they are ethnically matched demonstrates an affirmation of their religio-ethnic identity. With that in mind, it is important to examine this dynamic within the New Zealand context.

Religious Communities In New Zealand

While there has been a growing body of scholarship concerning church attendance in New Zealand, particularly the decline in institutional belonging evident in recent decades, very little of this has investigated the question of ethnicity.[48] There have been some attempts to address this issue, but nothing like the scholarly approaches we have already seen within overseas contexts. This section presents general observations from such literature. It provides a descriptive rather than instructive understanding of ethnic relations within religious communities of New Zealand.

The lack of research in this area is surprising given New Zealand's growing ethnic diversity. Since the signing of the Treaty of Waitangi between the British Crown and Māori chiefs in 1840, the vast majority of settlers in New Zealand were European. There were a few Chinese beginning in the 19th century, who came for the gold rush and chose to remain. In 1987 a major change in immigration policy enabled an increasing number of Asians from Korea, Hong Kong, Taiwan, Southeast Asia, India and China to settle in New Zealand. Those from various Pacific Islands nations began migrating in the early 20th century to support New Zealand's war efforts, and many more later followed in the 1960s and 1970s to sustain the labour force of a growing economy. Figures from the United Nations show that New Zealand has the highest percentage of its population who are immigrants of any country in the world, with 24% (in Australia this is 23%, and Canada follows closely with 22%).[49]

New Zealand is no longer a country mainly populated by European New Zealanders with pockets of other ethnicities. In 1961, New Zealand's population was 92% European and seven percent Māori, with Asian and Pacific Islanders sharing the remaining one percent. Between 2001 and 2006, Europeans decreased from 80% to 67.6% of the population. At the same time, the number of Pacific Islanders increased by almost 5%, while Asians experienced significant growth of nearly 50%.[50] Population projections suggest that by 2026 Europeans will decrease to 62%, while Māori and Asians will increase to 15% and Pacific Islanders to nine percent.[51] These figures demonstrate that the face of New Zealand society is changing rapidly. But what might these changes tell us about the ethnic and cultural characteristics of religious groups within the New Zealand context?

Analysing data from the 1996 census, the Christian Research Association of Aotearoa New Zealand found that the number of specific ethnicities identified for each religious group revealed the multi-ethnic nature of the groups. For example, within the Exclusive Brethren fourteen ethnicities were identified; but 174 ethnicities were noted within the Catholic Church.[52] Yet when prioritising specific ethnic identities into broader ones, such as European, Māori, Asian or Pacific Islander, the ethnic representation in some religious groups made them appear very homogeneous.[53] To illustrate this, the Exclusive Brethren consisted almost entirely of Europeans (99%); similar proportions are evident for Māori religions such a Ratana (96%) and Ringatu (98%), as well as Sikhism (96% Asian) and the Congregational Church (89% Pacific Islanders).[54] What we see from these figures is that some religious communities tend to be over-represented by a particular ethnic group. This suggests that people's religious and ethnic identities can be so closely intertwined that they confine their religious involvement among their own kind.

Although some of the non-Christian religions in New Zealand are relatively recent arrivals, faiths like Sikhism and Buddhism have been present in New Zealand society since the 19th century.[55] Looking at census figures, Todd Nachowitz notes that while there has been an overall decrease in the numbers of respondents stating adherence to a Christian denomination (a decrease of 11% since 1991), other religions with significant populations are showing substantial gains, especially Buddhism (+311%), Hinduism (+257%), and Islam (+492%).[56] Despite the decrease in the number of people affiliating with the Christian faith, the number of Asian Christians within the population increased from 3.2% in 2001 to 4.8% in 2006.[57] These Asian Christians have been found in faith communities largely consisting of their own people. Moreover, new migrant populations are seen to be responsible for the increases in other non-Christian religions, making those groups also more ethnic-specific in representation.[58]

Some religious communities did show signs of diversity. Groups from the 1996 census such as Jehovah's Witness, Assemblies of God, Seventh Day Adventist, and Mormon indicated diversity in terms of their ethnic representation.[59] The greater ethnic diversity within these communities suggests that their members might be inclined to embrace a more common religious identity rather than upholding a particular ethnic identity as their priority. The higher representation of Māori and Pacific Islanders within these religious groups may be, as Peter Lineham suggests, a consequence of "cultural patterns that were more expressive and less intellectual, and therefore closer to Polynesian culture," as well as a failure "to attract New Zealand European elite."[60] Even within the Baha'i faith, because of its principle of the unity of humankind, an "international multi-cultural character" is reflected in its affiliates and further enhanced through "the variety of marriages between different nationalities and races."[61]

Ethnic representation within some mainline Christian denominations also showed some level of diversity. The Methodist Church demonstrated more diversity in terms of ethnic representation than Catholic, Anglican, and Presbyterian denominations.[62] By 2006, the extent of ethnic diversity within these denominations had increased.[63] This was the result of the decline in the number of Europeans and the increased representations of the other main ethnic groups within the Anglican and Presbyterian denominations.[64] Even so, Europeans still remain the largest single ethnic group. This reflects their prominence in the general New Zealand population. But their increasing disassociation with religion has an impact, for the most part, on the Christian churches with which they traditionally aligned themselves.

Census data may show the ethnic representation of those who indicate an affiliation to religious groups in New Zealand, but they do not reflect how ethnic relations operate within them. With regard to some of the mainline Christian churches, a brief look at their organisational structures may provide a helpful picture of how this dynamic is worked out. Catholics who live within the boundary of a particular parish usually become part of the worshipping community of that parish. Therefore, the ethnic composition of a parish will depend on the ethnic representation of practicing Catholics within its bounds. There is uncertainty regarding ethnic representation in Mass attendance as parishes are not asked to keep those statistics.[65] Yet, according to Caritas, a social justice publication of the Catholic Church, "the experience of Auckland parishes is that there is a rapidly changing face to their congregations, while South Island parishes remain relatively isolated from sudden changes."[66]

The Anglican Church in Aotearoa New Zealand and Polynesia expresses ethnic and cultural relations in more clear-cut structural ways. In recognising the special relationship Māori have with the Crown through the Treaty of Waitangi, the General Synod/Te Hinota Whanui adopted a revised constitution in 1992 providing an opportunity for partnership between its three main ethnic groupings – Māori, Pakeha (European), and Pacific Islander. Each of the three partners is known as a *"tikanga"* (way, style, or cultural model) that works in ways to express itself as an equal partner in the decision-making process of the General Synod, and to exercise mission and ministry to God's people within its own cultural framework.[67]

There is a degree of autonomy for all three tikanga which encourages them to develop their own identities by culturally relevant means. With the adoption of this constitution, the Church of the Province of New Zealand became The Anglican Church in Aotearoa, New Zealand and Polynesia/Te Hahi Mihinare ki Aotearoa ki Niu Tireni, ki Nga Moutere o te Moana Nui a Kiwa.[68] It is uncertain how ethnically diverse or homogeneous Anglican congregations are, but it seems as though the equal-partner model operates in ways that affirm the distinct cultural identities of its members. This suggests that most congregations are likely to consist of people of a particular ethnic group.

The Methodist Church of New Zealand / Te Haahi Weteriana O Aotearoa also builds on the Treaty of Waitangi's spirit of partnership. It organises itself in terms of Synods reflecting greater distinctions between its main ethnic groups. There is Te Taha Māori (Māori), Synods (European), Sinoti Samoa (Samoan), and Vahefonua Tonga 'o Aotearoa (Tongan).[69] Bosi ko Viti kei Rotuma e Niusiladi (Fiji) is an "Advisory Committee."[70] Each of these bodies provides a forum where concerns relating to its members can be shared. Therefore, the membership of these bodies tends to be ethnically homogeneous. They seek primarily to meet the religio-cultural needs of their respective members and, from within that framework, to work in relationship with other bodies within the Methodist Conference. All of these Synods have regional boundaries or Districts, except for that of Tongans, which has national coverage for its membership.[71]

There has been an attempt at research looking specifically at ethnically diverse congregations in New Zealand. The Christian Research Association produced a kitset for congregations to reflect on their life in light of the challenge of having people of different ethnicities in their midst.[72] It presents experiences of what is described as "self-studies" by a very small sample of congregations and therefore provides a limited indication of what diverse congregations are really like. The research does, however, highlight issues related to the difficulties of cross-cultural interaction between different ethnic groups in congregations. For example, in one Presbyterian congregation that consisted of various European and Pacific Islander nationalities, it was identified that "learning to understand and work with people of another cultural background takes time."[73] Within a Catholic Church and with regard to Mass in specific languages, when the religious and cultural aspirations of people are not met by their local congregation, people would often travel to other congregations that could cater for their specific needs.[74]

What these self-studies highlight is that although a congregation may be ethnically diverse, the ways in which sub-groups organise themselves within it can demonstrate homogeneous tendencies. Despite the need for particular ethnic groups to meet together, the self-studies also recognise the need for groups to be mindful of the congregation's wellbeing as a whole. Therefore, there seems to be room in a congregation for particular religio-cultural expressions of Christian fellowship, but such expressions should also contribute to (and not be in isolation from) the wider congregational expression of itself.

We have seen that the very limited literature about ethnic relations within religious communities of New Zealand is primarily based upon census statistics rather than research in these communities. The scant material we do have is nonetheless helpful in conveying that ethnicity does matter. It shapes the way people organise themselves in religious communities. In most of them, people appear to live out their faith along ethnic and cultural lines, in preference for their own kind. This is clearly exemplified in Christian denominations such as Anglican and Methodist, where the relational life of members is exercised through ethnic-specific bodies (synods and tikanga). At the local level, then, religious communities tend to be ethnically homogeneous.

Conclusion

The literature we have examined conveys that ethnicity matters to people. It is important enough that they generally prefer to relate with others who share the same ethnicity and culture. Homogeneity builds a sense of solidarity that affirms identity and cultural norms. Since religion can be a core value alongside ethnic and cultural identity, people may often choose to express their religious affiliations in ethnic-specific ways. This is exemplified in the fact that, despite contexts such as that of New Zealand and the United States becoming increasingly diverse, most of their religious communities are largely homogeneous. It seems that ethnic diversity in the general population of a country or religious tradition does not necessarily translate into diversity within specific communities. We can conclude, then, that ethnicity plays a significant part in how people organise themselves in their congregations.

The ethnic relationship between clergy and congregation members has also been important to consider. It has been largely taken for granted that the ethnic homogeneity of a congregation includes that of the minister. Yet there is next to nothing in terms of research to prove this point. On the basis of the body of literature, I believe that my exploration within my own church tradition will reveal a tendency for both ministers and parishioners to be ethnically and culturally matched.

We have seen how prevalent ethnically homogeneous religious communities are. But from a Christian perspective, a fundamental question must be asked, "What is the theological basis for being church?" Moreover, how can our theology of church inform the issue of ethnic relations? We shall address these questions in the next chapter.

2 – An Ecclesiology of Unity in Diversity

Our ecclesiology or theological understanding of the church is imperative. In the previous chapter, we noted the prevalence of ethnically homogeneous religious communities and their tendency to organise themselves in ethnic-specific ways. But is there a theological basis for this? Christian communities, therefore, need to understand who and what they are. We can discern this by examining a variety of biblical texts. This deserves attention because exploring such texts provides a theological foundation upon which Christians, regardless of ethnicity and culture, can build community together in the church. They are important because they highlight not only the unity of the church, but also its diversity. We will explore a Christological and a Trinitarian ecclesiology that affirms the church's unity in diversity and then use them as a framework to examine how the PCANZ understands itself.

A Christological Perspective of the Church

A Christological understanding of the church sees the relationship between Christians as being grounded in their relationship with Christ. It is a relationship that has the effect of unifying the earthly and the divine. Because of this, unity among believers in the church is so important that any dissension is strongly discouraged. The Apostle Paul in 1 Corinthians 1:10 gives a warning against divisions and instead encourages the church's unity in Christ:

> "Now I appeal to you, brothers and sisters, by the name of our Lord Jesus Christ, that all of you should be in agreement and that there should be no divisions among you, but that you should be united in the same mind and the same purpose."

These words were addressed to a largely Gentile church with some Jewish Christians, but the appeal for unity among its members does not appear to be a result of any strife or tension in terms of ethnic relations.[75] Rather, Paul's call for unity is in response to the divisive tendency of some in the church who were loyal to certain teachings and leadership.[76]

Despite the differing opinions and practices about leadership and the gifts of the Spirit in the church at Corinth, Paul emphasised the corporate nature of Christ as fundamental to the nature of the church: "For just as the body is one and has many members, and all the members of the body, though many, are one body, so it is with Christ" (1 Corinthians 12:12). Since Christ is the one Lord of believers in the church, this understanding becomes the basis of their common life together. Through Christ, those in the church are bound together, "forming a corporate entity."[77] However, if faith in Christ cannot enable Christians to relate together corporately in the Church, then not preserving the unity of the church "means to deny that there is one Lord."[78]

Believers' union in Christ thus provides the basis for their unity in the church. Putting aside members' ethnicities, it is their belief and union in Christ that validates their fellowship with each other. Looking back to our earlier scenario at First Church, it would seem that, irrespective of the ethnic and cultural differences between the members of the congregation, their Christian identity is the foundation of their fellowship together in worship. If this is so, then language, perhaps, should not really be an issue. The problem, however, is that people's spiritual unity in Christ has to be lived out in practical ways. Therefore, how Christian unity is expressed by congregation members of different backgrounds is crucial for our understanding. Can their fellowship together truly be a sign of Christian unity when one group is allowed to uphold their cultural priority while others are denied theirs? If the answer is not in the affirmative, then having completely separate worship services under one roof without any fellowship together cannot really testify to their unity in Christ. Relying purely on a spiritual connection without any concrete manifestation of this belief is a "dead" faith (James 2:17).

People's relationship in Christ is one that transcends various boundaries. According to Galatians 3:28, based on an ancient baptismal formula, all are one in Christ without distinction of race, social status or sex: "There is no longer Jew or Greek, there is no longer slave or free, there is no longer male and female; for all of you are one in Christ Jesus."[79] Yet Paul's letter was addressed to converts who were formerly Gentile pagans (4:8-9). Recalling the essence of their unity through baptism, Paul attempts to dissuade the Galatian Christians from the teaching of Jewish Christian missionaries who were preaching "a different gospel" (1:6). They were arguing that Gentiles who had believed in Jesus should take the next step into full covenant membership, as Jewish Christians did, by adopting Jewish practices like circumcision (5:2-4; 6:12-13). Such practices were once identity markers that kept Jews separated from Gentiles. But Paul argues that for those who are part of the new community "in Christ" such markers are annulled, thereby emphasising their unity rather than their separation.

The implication of such an understanding is that in this baptismal formula "Jews and Gentiles are constituted together as one new people of God."[80] "To be sure, the Christians themselves soon came to believe that they constituted a *third race*, but this was only to show that in fact it was a 'non-racial race,' a *people* who, while claiming to be the true Israel, declared at the same time they did not care about the difference between a Greek and a Jew once these were members of the Christian Church."[81] The church was understood as a new people whose parameters could extend and permeate the existing ethnic and cultural boundaries and barriers of other peoples to include them. From this line of reasoning, the church as a "new creation" in Christ (Galatians 6:15; 2 Corinthians 5:17) can incorporate a diversity of ethnicities.

Although being "one in Christ Jesus" transcends ethnic and cultural distinctions of people in the church, it does not negate them. Considering the Apostle Paul's view of the Christian community, his prescription for the church's identity does not necessarily abolish particularism; instead, it simply erects, in place of an ethnic particularism, "an ecclesial particularism defined by faith in Christ."[82] This means that rather than disqualifying the ethnic, social, and gender identities of Christians, these distinctions are no longer of primary importance for their status as believers together in the church.[83]

As a consequence, not only does union with Christ enable people to be connected with each other and to come together as church, it also enables diverse peoples to do so. This Christian fellowship, as Moltmann argues, is a "fundamentally open fellowship" where a person is recognised in his or her otherness, and "it is only this recognition which makes it possible for people who are different to live together – Jews and Greeks, masters and slaves, men and women."[84] This means that, from a Christological perspective, there is diversity within the unity of people in the church.

To put this another way, not only does people's union in Christ create unity in the church, but that unity is also characterised by diversity. Again, when reconsidering our earlier scenario, the ethnic and cultural distinctions among people in the congregation need to be acknowledged and valued in their common fellowship together. Moltmann's point about an open fellowship would mean that the unity of those in the congregation should be inclusive not only of those who are different, but also of that which makes them different. This means the inclusion of their cultural elements, such as language.

With regard to Galatians 3:28, a coming together of diverse people as followers of Christ implies a sense of equality. "What is being claimed here is not only equal validity, but also equal being in Christ; not only equality in faith before God, but also equality in fellowship of Christ; not only equal pardon, but also equal rights."[85] For Moltmann, equality enables people in the church to recognise each other in their "human dignity" and "human rights."[86] This means that the diverse nature of the Church is reflective of the wider community of humanity. Such a fellowship of Christians would encourage ethnic diversity in representation, where they "no longer have to justify themselves on the basis of their own characteristics," which in turn encourages a fellowship of the "unequal and different, held together by free and courteous recognition."[87] If this is true, then the church is not meant to be a homogeneous community consisting purely of people who are the same: Jews with Jews, Greeks with Greeks, rich with rich, and so on. This is not to say that people of the same ethnicity cannot fellowship together in the church, but that a Christological ecclesiology is about unity, not uniformity. It is primarily about unity in diversity, not homogeneity.

When we revisit our earlier scenario, the notion of unity rather than uniformity in Christ would argue for a diverse way in which people relate together in the congregation. This includes the language or languages used in worship. When people recognise and value others (who are ethnically and culturally different) as equals in Christ, then equality should also extend to the inclusion of these others' languages. Their fellowship together in worship is a shared experience, rather than one in which the cultural elements of a particular group override those of others.

Being one in Christ not only enables people in the church to recognise each other as equals while valuing their otherness, but such a relationship also means accepting one another in fellowship. Romans 15:7, 13 states, "Welcome one another, therefore, just as Christ has welcomed you, for the glory of God ... May the God of hope fill you with all joy and peace in believing, so that you may abound in hope by the power of the Holy Spirit." The Greek word for "welcome" can also be translated as "accept" or "receive." These were words addressed to both Gentile and Jewish Christians of the first-century church in Rome who were experiencing tense relations within their fellowship.[88] They also highlight that the basis of their acceptance of each other was Christ's acceptance of them.

Again, for Moltmann, acceptance of one another in the church is being truly faithful to Christ's acceptance of them, particularly when they can accept those who are different.[89] It is so crucial to a congregation's life that Moltmann describes acceptance as "the atmosphere of humanity. Where acceptance is lacking, the air becomes thin, our breathing falters, and we languish."[90] Therefore, a real sense of life or vitality in a congregation that is based on acceptance can be truly tested within an ethnically diverse context.

Acceptance of one another in the church is also testimony to the reconciliatory act of Christ. Ephesians 2:14 presents Christ as the one who has broken down "the dividing wall" between peoples to reconcile them with God and each other. It is thought that the Ephesians letter may not be addressing a local community; rather, here the vision of the church is set in the largest possible framework (universal) where the body of all the faithful is united with the risen

Christ as its head (1:22-23; 2:6).[91] Although Ephesians highlights the incorporation of Gentiles with Israel (2:11-12), there does not appear to be any indication that the distinction created a problem for relationships between Jewish and Gentile Christians in their unity. The idea of Christ abolishing "the law with its commandments and ordinances" seems to be conveyed without difficulty, which suggests that the churches to which the letter was written probably did not include an active Jewish Christian group.[92]

The point is that by accepting Christ in faith, Gentiles become part of God's people, Israel, and share in God's promises to them. This reconciliation at a faith level provides the basis for ethnic relations to be worked out in reality within and between local congregations. Therefore, regardless of whether a congregation is ethnically homogeneous, it has a theological foundation upon which to develop diversity within the unified body of Christ. Relations between diverse peoples can be developed while they "with all humility and gentleness, with patience, bearing with one another in love, [make] every effort to maintain the unity of the Spirit in the bond of peace. There is one body and one Spirit, just as you were called to the one hope of your calling, one Lord, one faith, one baptism, one God and Father of all, who is above all and through all and in all" (4:1-6). This is an appeal to Christians to fulfil their "calling" to a "worthy" way of living together in the Church and to become what it should be through the "unifying realities of the faith."[93]

When applying the above view of acceptance to our earlier scenario, we can see that a genuine acceptance of one another in Christ means living out Christ's acceptance of all in the congregation. Although one group had been in the congregation before others, Christ's reconciliatory work enables people who were once apart to be in fellowship together. Their acceptance of each other and relations together in the church, despite ethnic and cultural differences, is based primarily upon the authority of Christ's love, acceptance, and reconciliation for them, not upon the rights or privileges of those who were first in the congregation. According to Ephesians 4:1-6 the unity of people in the church is not something to be attained. Rather, in Christ, it is presupposed; those in the congregation, through humility, gentleness, and patience, are to find ways of maintaining or exercising that unity in peace. The acceptance and incorporation of the languages of its respective ethnic groups in a joint worship service is a way of contributing to the whole fellowship, rather than purely catering to the needs of some.

Texts from the Gospels also speak of the relations among the followers of Jesus and with God. Although the accounts of Jesus' life are thought to be written later than that of Paul's early epistles, they still provide insights into the understanding of early Christians about their relations amongst each other within their communities.[94] Matthew 18:20 records Jesus saying: "For where two or three are gathered in my name, I am there among them." These words are from a section (18:15-20) that uses the term "church" or "ecclesia," which indicates the influence of an early Christian community upon the Gospel account.[95] They also appear to echo a rabbinic belief that if two sit together and words of the Law are between them, the *Shekinah* (God's presence) rests between them.[96]

However, for the followers of Jesus the divine presence among them is now Jesus himself. Although this section uses the numbers "two" and "three" as a way of affirming their fellowship, it is clear that their unity as a church is constituted by the presence of Christ. From this, and from inferences from the epistles, it can be seen that a Christological approach to the church is one where Christ initiates relations between its members. Whatever the concerns affecting the relations between Christians in the congregation, they are Christ's community when they participate together in the presence of Christ.

Another Gospel text that talks about the unity of Christians in relation to the unity of God is Jesus' prayer for his disciples in John 17:21-23. Here Jesus prays that

> they may all be one. As you Father are in me and I am in you, may they also be in us, so that the world may believe that you have sent me. The glory you have given me I have given them, so that they may be one as we are one. I in them and you in me, that they may become completely one, so that the world may know that you have sent me and have loved them even as you have loved me.

Again, it can be seen that the followers of Jesus are perceived to be "completely one" in their relationship with each other when based upon their relationship with Jesus who, in turn, is in relationship with the Father. "Any approach that places the essence of unity in the solidarity of human endeavour is not really faithful to John's insistence that unity has its origins in divine action."[97] This does not imply passivity on behalf of the followers of Jesus; rather, the unity has to be visible enough to challenge the world to believe in Jesus. Since the world includes people of different ethnicities and cultural backgrounds, and since Christianity had spread from Jewish Palestine into the Gentile regions of the Mediterranean, the unity within and between the various Christian communities had to reflect this unity in Christ. According to Gail O'Day, "The unity for which Jesus prays is not intrinsic to the community itself, but derives from the primal unity of Father and Son. For the community to be 'one' means that they mirror the mutuality and reciprocity of the Father/Son relationship."[98] Therefore, the unity of the community of believers is a witness to the unity and community of God.

These Gospel texts also support the unity and good relations of people in our First Church scenario. If Christ's presence constitutes the unity of the respective ethnic groups in their worship, then it must also constitute their respective languages used for worship. A common language may be helpful in some ways in the life of the church, but if it benefits only some while disadvantaging others its witness to Christ's unifying presence in the congregation is very limiting. Instead, this dynamic may convey that some of the practices of particular groups in the church are more acceptable or preferable than others. Worse still is the idea that Christ might prefer some groups and their cultural practices over others. But Christ's presence in the church means that Christ lived and died for all, not just for some.

These are just a sampling of biblical texts that indicate a Christological basis for being the church. They clearly show how a Christological ecclesiology emphasises the unity of believers in Christ while accepting the diversity of believers in the church. The Christian church is therefore one, yet many, in terms of its diversity at different levels. However, the diversity of local churches is not regarded as comprising the unity of the church as a whole. As Alister McGrath rightly points out, the church already possesses a unity through its common calling in Christ, "which expresses itself in different communities in different cultures and situations."[99] In this respect, unity must not be understood sociologically or organisationally, but theologically. Hans Küng calls attention to this point in his own study of the church when he states:

> To judge it by externals (canon law, ecclesiastical language, Church administration etc.) is to misunderstand it completely. The unity of the Church is a spiritual entity. It is not chiefly a unity of the members among themselves; it depends finally not on itself but on the unity of God, which is efficacious through Jesus Christ in the Holy Spirit… The Church is one and therefore should be one.[100]

All of this is a useful beginning, but in order to gain a wider perspective to complement our understanding of what it means to be the church, a Trinitarian approach must now be considered.

A Trinitarian Perspective of the Church

It has been established that the unity of the church is grounded in the reconciliatory work of God through Jesus Christ. But since Christianity's understanding of God incorporates a Trinitarian view of the Father, Son and Holy Spirit, this view must also contribute to an understanding of the church. Some of the texts examined thus far have already implied the inclusion of the Trinity with respect to ecclesiology. A further exploration of some of these texts and others will make this perspective more explicit.

Christianity affirms the unity of God. In both the Old and New Testaments (Deuteronomy 6:4; Mark 12:29-30), God is accepted as being "one" or the only God. But the Gospels make it very clear that in Jesus Christ there is a relationship in God reflected through the Father and the Son in which God the Father sent Jesus the Son into the world. This relationship is very openly conveyed in John 17. But also at work through Jesus is the Holy Spirit (John 14:15-17, 25-26; 16:7-8, 13-15). The account of Jesus' baptism in the Synoptic Gospels (Matthew 3:16-17; Mark 1:9-11; Luke 3:21-22) highlights this divine dynamic of these three elements. Perhaps the most explicit Trinitarian text, which is again tied to the idea of baptism, is Matthew 28:19: "Go then to all nations and make them my disciples: baptize them in the name of the Father, the Son, and the Holy Spirit."

The epistles of the New Testament also bear witness to the Trinitarian concept of God. Such passages testify to the pervasive pattern of divine activity, where God's saving presence and power can, it would seem, be expressed only by involving all three elements:

> "But when the goodness and loving kindness of God our Saviour appeared, he saved us, not because of any works of righteousness that we had done, but according to his mercy, through the water of rebirth and renewal by the Holy Spirit. This Spirit is poured out on us richly through Jesus Christ our Saviour" (Titus 3:4-6).[101]

As in Matthew 28:19, used in the baptism formula of the church, 2 Corinthians 13:14 is also a formula in Christian prayer and devotion that highlights a Trinitarian understanding of God in the church: "The grace of our Lord Jesus Christ, the love of God, and the fellowship of the Holy Spirit be with you all."

The doctrine of God as triune is one that is grounded in the idea of community. A classical Trinitarian understanding of God is "one in essence, distinguished in three persons." Such a view was, in part, to guard against the misunderstandings of subordinationalism (ranks of order of deity), modalism (mere masks of God's being), and tritheism (individual and separate deities).[102] In essence, these concepts were attempts to portray God in light of the event of Jesus Christ and the outpouring of the Holy Spirit. For Daniel Migliore, the triune God is essentially a communion of persons in love, whereby God is "self-expending, other-affirming, community-building love."[103] Moreover, the Trinitarian persons are not isolated and independent selves but have their personal identity in relationship. To confess that God is triune is to affirm that God exists in community. As such, Migliore again asserts that community is also God's will for people.[104] Therefore, the Trinitarian understanding of God as community is fundamental to the understanding of the church as those who relate together in community.

The distinctiveness of the triune persons suggests that God is a diverse community. It is a communion of the different. Just as a Christological perspective accepts the "otherness" of others in Christ, so it is within the community of the Trinity. The relationship between the three elements of Father, Son and Holy Spirit and their unity has been described as "perichoresis." The concept of perichoresis was hinted at by some of the early church fathers, such as Irenaeus and Tertullian, and developed further by Gregory of Nyssa.[105] Perichoresis allows the individuality of the persons in God to be maintained, while insisting that each person shares in the life of the other two.

An image often used to express this idea is that of "community of being," in which each person of the Trinity, while maintaining its distinctive identity, penetrates the others and is penetrated by them. In John 10:37-38, Jesus declared his relationship with God to those who found it difficult to accept: "If I am not doing the works of my Father, then do not believe me. But if I do them, even though you do not believe me, believe the works, so you may know and understand that the Father is in me and I am in the Father." Though distinct from each other, the persons of the Trinity can only truly be themselves when in relationship with each other.

> The one divine person is not only itself, but rather carries within itself also the other divine persons, and only in this indwelling of the other persons within it is it the person it really is. The Son is Son only insofar as the Father and Spirit indwell him; without this interiority of the Father and Spirit, there would be no Son. The same applies to the Father and to the Spirit. [106]

The implication of such an intertwined divine relationship is that one cannot be acknowledged without the others – hence Jesus' remark, "Whoever has seen me has seen the Father" (John 14:9).

This follows on to another understanding of the triune relationship as being one of "appropriation." Appropriation maintains that the works of the Trinity are a unity; every person of the Trinity is involved in every outward action of God. For example, the Father, Son and Holy Spirit are all involved in the work of creation although it is understood to be the distinctive work of the Father; this is likewise true regarding the work of redemption, although this is primarily seen as the distinctive work of the Son. Taken together, the doctrines of perichoresis and appropriation allow us to think of God as a "community of being," in which all is shared, united, and mutually exchanged.

> Father, Son, and Spirit are not three isolated and diverging compartments of the Godhead, like three subsidiary components of an international corporation. Rather, they are differentiations within

the Godhead, which become evident within the economy of salvation and the human experience of redemption and grace. The doctrine of the Trinity affirms that beneath the surface of the complexities of the history of salvation and our experience of God, lies one God, and one God only. [107]

Taking into account our triune understanding of God, a Trinitarian ecclesiology would encourage diversity in the church. To be in relationship with the triune God, people in the church would be in relationship with others who are different from them. Their common identity as people "in Christ" is the basis for their unity in the church and this is complemented further by the dynamic of their diversity. Their relations with each other are such that not even their respective distinctiveness of ethnicity or cultural status should prevent their unity and their sharing in each other's life. Therefore, a Trinitarian ecclesiology, like that of a Christological ecclesiology, sees the church as a community in which there is unity in diversity.

At the same time, just as metaphors for the church such as "body" have their limitations, so too do any comparisons of the divine relations with human ones. Because human persons cannot be internal to one another as subjects, their unity cannot be conceived in a strictly perichoretic fashion. [108] In re-evaluating Jesus' prayer for his disciples, "As you, Father, are in me and I am in you, may they also be in us" (John 17:23), Volf argues that human perichoretic unity does not necessarily follow from divine perichoretic unity, except that believers have a common life together because of their life in the unity of God. [109] Jesus did not pray "may they be *in each other*;" rather "may they be *in us*."

The rationale follows that since the Son dwells in human beings through the Spirit, then the unity of the church is grounded upon the indwelling of the Spirit, who is in a perichoretic unity with the other divine persons. The Holy Spirit is the "one person in many persons." [110] It is therefore not the mutual perichoresis of human beings, but rather the permeation of the Spirit common to everyone that makes the church into a communion corresponding to the Trinity. It is a communion in which personhood and relations are equal. Just as God constitutes human beings through their social and natural relations as independent persons, so also does the

Holy Spirit through Christ living in them constitute them through church relations as an intimate communion of independent persons. Relations among diverse people in the church are not only possible, but they also involve a mutual sharing of each other that affirms their being together.

> In this mutual giving and receiving, we give to others not only something, but also a piece of ourselves, something of that which we have made of ourselves in communion with others; and from others we take not only something, but also a piece of them. Each person gives of himself or herself to others, and each person in a unique way takes up others into himself or herself. This is the process of mutual internalization of personal characteristics occurring in the church through the Holy Spirit indwelling Christians.[111]

This way of relating with one another through the Spirit opens them up to one another and allows them to recognise, appreciate and accept other Christians in their uniqueness. The fellowship of the Holy Spirit is experienced by those who know it as both the love that binds and the freedom that provides the space for relations between Christians to work out together.

> Love confers that which is held in common, freedom opens up the scope of what is individual and singular. Both aspects must be noted when we are talking about the fellowship of the life-giving Spirit. Without freedom, love crushes the diversity of what is individual; without love, freedom destroys what is shared and binds us together. Community which serves life can therefore only be understood as integrating, and as creating unity in diversity, while at the same time differentiating and making diversity possible. The unity of this unity and this diversity is to be found in *the rhythm of the times* of life. We call this *the Trinitarian fellowship* of the Spirit.[112]

Based on what we know now about a Trinitarian ecclesiology, we should revisit our earlier scenario to see how it might help us to respond to the tension within the congregation. The distinction of each person in the Trinity validates the distinction of each ethnic group in the congregation. But since the essence of the triune God is its unity in community, rather than the individual distinction of each divine person, then this must also be reflected in the congregation. The church in essence is also a community of peoples in which its corporate life and identity is central to its being. The way the divine persons interrelate (perichoresis) indicates that there should be an interrelation, a sharing, a giving and receiving amongst all ethnic groups. This includes not only the physical space to allow the groups to fellowship together, but also an incorporation of their respective languages that demonstrates their shared life together.

Embracing a Christological and Trinitarian ecclesiology, then, encourages the view of unity in diversity for the Christian church. They are not entirely independent of each other in terms of how we understand the God upon whom the church is grounded. Our ecclesiologies would also encourage each group of the congregation in our story to be gracious in its relations with others who are different from them, so that their unity is preserved and can be worked out in more constructive ways. This is a graciousness that actively engages with others to bring purpose to their life as a whole community of God while respecting their distinctive characteristics. This is also applicable to the Church on earth as a whole. It is in this kind of fellowship that the church, in a human way, corresponds to the diverse fellowship and catholicity of the divine persons of the Godhead. It also indicates a relationship between the local and universal church. Exploring this relationship may further help our understanding of ethnic relations in the church.

The Universal and Local Church

Examining Christological and Trinitarian approaches to ecclesiology clearly affirms the unity in diversity of those in the church. These approaches have also informed the Church's understanding of itself through its statements of faith or creeds. The earliest church creeds such as the Nicene (325 C.E.) and, perhaps earlier still, the Apostles' (second century), included words that marked or characterised the church as "one," "holy," "catholic" and "apostolic."[113] Such descriptions were marks or defining characteristics of the church and came about as attempts to unify the church in response to doctrinal schisms rather than ethnic or cultural ones.

The idea of the church as being "one" and "catholic" puts an emphasis on its unity. The mark of being "catholic" means that the church is whole or complete in the sense that it is present in all parts of the world, through all periods of history, and includes all kinds of people.[114] Believers in Christ who have died can be thought of as the invisible Church in a heavenly sense, while the church on earth can be considered in a visible way in the local setting. We noted earlier how Küng saw the visible and invisible church as positively being "one," and as such he also viewed it as a "spiritual entity" where people's union in Christ and each other transcends time and space. The invisible church in the heavenly realm can, therefore, be seen as consisting of people from all over the world over time. It is the church in unity and diversity. But is it realistic at the earthly or local level?

It may be helpful to clarify further what is meant when using the term "local." The word "ecclesia" is quite naturally used in the plural in the New Testament and linked with place-names, which in some cases describe different worlds: Jerusalem and Corinth, Antioch and Rome. There is, then, a multiplicity of local churches (those of Ephesus, Philippi, Thessalonica, etc.), in which the one church manifests itself: the churches of individual towns and villages. There is also a multiplicity of regional churches (the church in Judea, Galilee and Samaria, Galatia, Macedonia, Asia Minor, etc.), in which the one church is also present: the churches of individual provinces (presbytery or diocese, depending on the denomination). This view of the local church can include a national body or the church of a continent.

Finally, there is a multiplicity of different types of churches (the Hellenistic, the Judaeo-Christian, etc.), which often coincide with regional churches but which are also at times, as a result of population movements, dispersed throughout different regions: the churches of different rites or denominations.[115] In this sense, the local church as the visible church on earth involves numerous churches in terms of tradition or denomination represented at different levels.[116] Taken together from different places and populations, these churches form a diverse collective.

Churches can also reflect the population in which they are located. Whether at the congregational, regional or national levels, churches have the potential to be ethnically homogeneous. Because the unity of the church presupposes a multiplicity of churches, "the various churches do not need to deny their origins of their specific situations; their language, their history, their customs and traditions, their way of life and thought, their personal structure will differ fundamentally, and no one has the right to take this from them. The same thing is not suitable for everyone, at every time and in every place."[117]

The understanding here is that churches (in the wider sense), consisting largely of a particular ethnic group and expressing their faith through culturally relevant ways, are valid churches in their own right. Moreover, their legitimacy is affirmed when they confess their unity with other ethnically different churches in the wider body of Christ in the world. It is the distinctiveness of the respective churches within the corporate body that enables their unity and diversity. If we were to view the church on earth as a whole, then, the combination of distinctive homogeneous churches, whether as a national body or denomination, would make the church appear very diverse.

However, we are more interested in ethnic relations at the local congregation level. As the visible fellowship of believers gathered in a specific location, the local congregation is perhaps the most concrete expression of the covenant people of God. But as we have seen above, the gathered congregation, at the same time, derives its significance from its participation in, and as the representation of, the whole church. If this is true, then each local congregation, because of its relationship with Christ and with others, can be thought of as nothing less than the reality of the one whole church. Each local congregation is the church of Jesus Christ "in miniature."[118] It reflects the spiritual connection with the wider church.

But this view raises some obvious questions. Is a local congregation meant to reflect the ethnic and cultural diversity of the wider church? Or can a congregation retain an ethnically homogeneous identity while remaining within the diversity of the wider church? The universal church is one because of its faith in Christ; it is also diverse because it includes all kinds of peoples from different places over time. Since it is one with the local church, it stands to reason that diversity is also to be demonstrated at the level of the local congregation. This is what a Christological and Trinitarian ecclesiology argues for. Tyron Inbody asserts that "any church, including a local congregation, which does not intend to be catholic in the sense that it invites all manner of people – people of differing sexes, races, classes, sexual orientation, national origin, intelligence, skills, even odors – is not the church."[119]

But, again, how realistic is this view? If an ethnically homogeneous congregation reflects the population in which it is located, does that necessarily disqualify it from being church because it is not diverse? It is difficult to imagine that churches consisting of a particular people in a specific place cannot be seen as churches on their own. This is especially so when people in such churches confess Christ and participate faithfully with others in the life of their congregation and in their regional or national bodies. Such congregations are largely homogeneous by default because their membership represents the population of their geographical area. It would hardly seem fair that such churches should be discredited as valid Christian communities. They cannot, after all, seek to become ethnically diverse when the homogeneity of their population limits this possibility.

Yet there can be a scope of variation within a homogeneous context. Ethnicity, of course, is only one dimension. It might be argued that if we consider the other identity markers of Galatians 3:28 (slave/free and male/female) we can see that there are differences between people in a much wider sense of catholicity for the church. If those in the faith community are accepted by Christ as the people they are, then surely they have a right to be the church where they are and as they are. This would have to apply not only to congregations but to regional, national, or denominational church bodies as well.

It may be tempting to think so. But again, if the unity among homogeneous churches is simply "spiritual" (in terms of Christian identity) without interactive fellowship (to reflect the perichoresis dynamic of the Trinity), then is this really unity? Rather than unity, this dynamic can perhaps be seen as a form of ecclesial segregation. This may be especially true considering the modern, pluralistic, global and transient world communities today. If so, then this dynamic cannot be what a Christological and Trinitarian ecclesiology affirms.

What, then, do we say about churches in places where there is an ethnic diversity of Christians with the potential of being together in a congregation? Does our understanding of ecclesiology encourage Christians to be part of ethnically diverse congregations, or does it encourage familiarity in distinctive fellowships? If we presume, all things being equal, that people have freedom of choice, what would influence their choice most? Would it be their ecclesiology or their ethnic and cultural preferences? To further contemplate these questions, I will narrow the discussion by applying it to the PCANZ.

Ethnic Relations Within the PCANZ

I wanted to understand how local congregations of my denomination, the PCANZ, organised themselves in terms of ethnic relations. This would help identify whether or not congregations ordered themselves in ways that were consistent with the ecclesiology of the PCANZ. It is therefore important first of all to gain some knowledge of how the PCANZ understands itself. We shall do this by considering two of its very important documents: the Book of Order[120] (BOO) and Kupu Whakapono.[121] The BOO is one that defines the self-understanding of the PCANZ. It explains the purpose, structures and offices, as well as the governance of the Church. Kupu Whakapono is the PCANZ's Confession of Faith, with a commentary that helps clarify its core beliefs about itself.

Each of these documents adopts both a Christological and Trinitarian ecclesiology in its self-understanding of the PCANZ. The Kupu Whakapono confesses that belief in Christ "restores us to God and one another."[122] Focusing on the reconciliatory work of Christ (Ephesians 2:14; 4:14-16), "the life to which we are called in Christ is a life in which divisions are overcome and enmity is brought to an end. Because of what God has done for us in Christ, we are called to reach out in love to others (2 Corinthians 5:16-21)."[123] This "reaching out in love to others" can be applied to those both inside and outside of the church. To those inside the church, the dynamic infers that there is an active reaching out to engage with others regardless of distinctions that might keep them separate. Therefore, if we apply this aspect to the PCANZ, we can see that it hopes to overcome divisive barriers amongst its members enabling them to be together in the church.

The PCANZ also believes that the unity of Christians is empowered through the Holy Spirit who "gathers us into the community of Christ."[124] As noted earlier in this chapter, it is a community that "reflects the loving interdependence within the triune being of God" and, as such, it also "transcends all boundaries of time, place, customs, race and culture."[125] As the Kupu Whakapono states, "We belong to this triune God, women and men, young and old, from many nations, in Christ *he iwi kotahi tatou* [we are one people]."[126] This clearly affirms the PCANZ understanding of the unity and diversity of the church, where distinctions between people are valued in their shared life together.

> Our unity in Christ does not imply a homogeneous church. Belonging to the triune God means we reflect the diversity inherent in God's own being and in the profusion of God's creation. The new creation that is God's new humanity in Christ is richly diverse: it is both Jew and Gentile, female and male, young and old, poor and rich. It represents a vast array of races, languages and cultures (Acts 2:5-11; Revelation 5:9). It includes people of a great variety of natural capacities and spiritual gifts (1 Corinthians 1:26; Romans 12:3-8; 1 Corinthians 12-14).[127]

> In Christ, the dividing walls of hostility are broken down (Ephesians 2:14), and, in Christ, believers are made one (Galatians 3:28). In Christ, diverse groups of people are brought together in a community of faith and love. The body of Christ thus reflects God's purpose to bring all things together in Christ (Ephesians 1:10), and is built up as a sign and anticipation of God's kingdom. It is only the power of the risen Christ and the work of the Holy Spirit which bring such reconciliation.[128]

The words "from many nations" acknowledge that the church is truly universal, multi-ethnic, multi-cultural, comprised of people of "every tribe and tongue," from every corner of the globe. The oneness in Christ brings great richness of fellowship and mutual learning. When applied to the context of the PCANZ, it affirms the Church's increasing enrichment by people who have come from many other places and cultures, including those of the Pacific and Asia.[129] With regard to Māori, the PCANZ embraces its bicultural relationship based upon the Treaty of Waitangi "that sought to honour both Māori and settlers as of equal status and rights."[130]

The PCANZ acknowledges that the unity among diverse peoples will be fully realised only in the oneness that is established in Christ.[131] Furthermore, the unity of the PCANZ "will have value only as it binds us together in the one body of Christ, as it nourishes the Church in mission, and as it renews confidence in and commitment to the saving grace of God in the life, death and resurrection of Jesus Christ."[132] The implication here, again, is that the unity of the church is made real through the concrete uniting practices of those involved. Words such as "binds," "nourishes" and "renews" indicate an active, not a passive, relationship. If the PCANZ confesses that "we belong to this triune God," then it is expected that the perichoretic inter-relations of the distinct persons of the Trinity will be reflected among the distinctive ethnic groups within the PCANZ.

We have seen that the PCANZ clearly understands itself to be a diverse Church that also exists in the wider unity and diversity of the universal church. Like Küng's view of the church as a "spiritual entity," the PCANZ also sees it as a "spiritual fellowship."[133] But in terms of an active unity, how is this "spiritual fellowship" worked out in real or concrete ways? How might ethnic relations operate at the different levels in which the PCANZ is represented – the global, national, regional and local congregation levels?

Relations at the Global Level

As part of the wider body of Christ, the PCANZ engages with other churches or Christian organisations in the world.[134] Its contribution to such organisations enables ethnic relations to work at both a Church-to-Church level and a personnel level through delegates represented at events of these global organisations. The PCANZ also has formalised partnerships with other churches. These include the Presbyterian Church of Vanuatu and the Presbyterian Church of Northern India. Therefore, it is part of the wider body of Christ; its relationship with other Churches and Christian organisations enables the PCANZ to live out its ecclesiology within a diverse global church. It is intentional and active through organisational, systemic and personnel processes enabling people of different ethnicities and cultures to engage together.

Relations at the National Level

The PCANZ also values unity and diversity within itself. We have noted above that it acknowledges a bicultural partnership with Māori. This partnership is expressed in the PCANZ between Te Aka Puaho and its other church courts.[135] The PCANZ also values its multicultural character through its members represented from nations around the world.[136] As such, the PCANZ considers itself a "cross-cultural" church through the "sharing of experiences, wisdom and learning from many different cultures."[137] It is committed to unity.[138]

The formation, inclusion and structural connections of national ethnic bodies within PCANZ, such as Te Aka Puaho, the Pacific Islanders Synod (later renamed the Pacific Presbytery), and the Council for Asian Congregations (see Chapter Three), further point to the PCANZ as an ethnically and culturally diverse organisation. The General Assembly is the highest court of the PCANZ that incorporates representations from its various national bodies, presbyteries and congregations. When the General Assembly meets every two years the unity and diversity of the PCANZ is most evident.

Unity and diversity are also revealed through representation on various national committees of the PCANZ. The Council of Assembly is a committee of the General Assembly whose primary function, amongst others, is to act on behalf of the General Assembly between Assemblies to consider and determine administrative issues relating to the Church.[139] The membership of the Council of Assembly must include one representative from each presbytery (which includes Te Aka Puaho and Pacific) and one "Asian/multicultural representative"[140] The same balance, where possible, is applied to the membership of the various subcommittees of the Council of Assembly.

It can be seen, then, that ethnic relations within the PCANZ are intentionally demonstrated through the diverse representation and consultative capacities of its various groups. From a systemic perspective, such representations and processes within the PCANZ recognise the importance of the ethnic/cultural identity of and relationships between its members. Perhaps it is also an attempt to reflect the growing diversity developing within other institutions of the wider New Zealand society. Therefore, national ethnic bodies within the PCANZ can be seen to manifest a working relationship between themselves.

The relationship of Te Aka Puaho with the courts of the Church reflects the relationship between the Crown and Māori based on the Treaty of Waitangi, and gives rise to similar responsibilities between those involved.[141] The main duty of Te Aka Puaho is to attend to the ministry needs of its pastorates and all who fall under its "*Maru*" or oversight.[142] By providing a "Māori cultural perspective" to the church's mission, Te Aka Puaho is represented on various committees of the PCANZ and is consulted about matters pertaining to the interests of Māori within PCANZ.[143]

For a significant part, the Asian component of PCANZ was largely dealt with by a group known as the Council for Asian Congregations. It's pan-Asian nature incorporated Chinese, Koreans, Indonesians, Taiwanese and Indians. Representation on the Council consisted of two people from each congregation (usually elders), including ministers (Asian or non-Asian) who are engaged in ministry to Asian people within the PCANZ.[144] This provided a setting for respective Asian groups to interact and make decisions together. As a way of further encouraging relations the Council rotated the chairmanship, thereby promoting equality amongst the distinctive Asian groups.[145] Beyond the Council, relations with non-Asians within the PCANZ was usually exercised through the role of the Asian Liaison Officer, who was appointed as part of the General Assembly staff. This position is currently called the Asian Coordinator and is the face of the Asian component of the PCANZ (though not exclusively) to other bodies within the PCANZ. Non-Asians engaging with the Asian Coordinator may be seen as a form of diverse ethnic relations, but this capacity is very limited compared to engaging with Asian groups or congregations.

Despite these opportunities for engagement across ethnic and cultural lines, there is little evidence of inter-ethnic relations amongst the respective Asian nationalities as well as with the rest of the Church. The Council for Asian Congregations as a body was diverse in its pan-Asian representation and provided a forum for ethnic relations to form. But the ethnic and cultural homogeneity of its congregations leaves very few opportunities for engagement with other Asian and non-Asian congregations. Since Asian representation in the PCANZ has devolved from the Council of Asian Congregations to the Asian Coordinator, it is unclear how the ministry and relationship of Asian congregations with each other and the wider church are being organised.

There are similarities with the Pacific Presbytery, formerly the Pacific Islanders Synod, which is pan-Pacific in its representation. The way it organises itself, with respect to the different island-group constituencies, recognises the importance of ethnic relations. The Pacific Presbytery has island groups comprising of Cook Islanders, Niueans, Samoans, Tokelauans, and Tuvaluans. One of the purposes of the Synod is to "provide a forum within the Church for Pacific Islanders to meet and to share matters of common and special concern."[146] There is an intention to balance both the unity of its broad Pacific identity and the diversity of its respective cultural groups by encouraging "ethnic fellowships."[147] Each island group elects its own office bearers and organises its own meetings. To promote a sense of equality in recognition of its ethnic diversity, there is an endeavour for the moderatorship of the Presbytery to rotate among the island groups. It is an intentional effort to maintain a balance in the ethnic representation of its leadership.

However, apart from the Presbytery meetings, where representatives of each island group can engage together, it is less apparent between the island groups themselves. As already noted, if "ethnic fellowships" are encouraged, perhaps it is more likely that each island group will develop itself in ways that promote its own religious and cultural interests. This would make engagement between groups less of a priority.

When we apply a Christological or Trinitarian ecclesiology to ethnic relations within the PCANZ we can see that, at a national level, its structures and processes seek to facilitate unity in diversity. The ethnic and cultural distinctiveness of the respective people groups are acknowledged and they are encouraged to work in ways that further develop respective group identities as well as their collective identity. The intentional effort for representation on various committees and the rotation of leadership are examples of the interactive ways in which these groups exercise unity and diversity. But it should not be forgotten that these interactions are mainly by representatives of ethnic groups, not by groups as a whole. The operations of the groups remain largely within their respective homogeneous contexts. Therefore, although the unity and diversity of the PCANZ at the national level is happening and is intentional, it is somewhat limited.

Relations at the Regional Level

Diversity at the regional level is slightly less obvious. Presbyteries are the regional courts of the PCANZ and are primarily responsible to "resource the life, worship, spiritual nurture and mission of the congregations" in their areas.[148] The membership of a presbytery usually consists of ministers and appointed elders from the congregations in the presbytery area.[149] The BOO makes no significant mention of the ethnic representation of presbytery members; except that a minister of Te Aka Puaho in the bounds of that presbytery can also be a member of the presbytery.[150] The other exception is where "a church council may elect and commission more than one elder to serve as members of presbytery if the congregation includes two or more ethnic groups of over 50 members and each elder is a member of a separate ethnic group."[151] This statement is significant because it acknowledges the issue of ethnic representation in congregations, as well as how that might affect representation to the presbytery. Therefore, ethnic representation within a presbytery depends on the homogeneity or diversity of congregations represented in its area.

Presbyteries do not operate in isolation. Working with other presbyteries can include working with Te Aka Puaho and the Pacific Presbytery. Again, this is largely in a consultative capacity as members and clergy may serve together on committees or provide advice on certain issues. It is also a demonstration of respect for each other.

Relations at the Local Congregation Level

We have observed that at a regional level the presbyteries of the PCANZ have the potential to be ethnically diverse. This is dependent, however, upon the ethnic representation within their congregations. It is at the local congregational level where much is unknown about the unity and diversity of the Church.

Ethnic relations within the PCANZ at the local level are much more difficult to gauge. There is nothing in the BOO that specifically refers to ethnic matters in relation to membership, groups, structures or relationships within a congregation. It seems that the way a congregation organises itself is left to the congregation and its leadership to work out. Since ethnic diversity and relations of the PCANZ are recognisable at the global, national and regional levels, one might expect this to be reflected at the congregational level. One might also expect that, since the PCANZ's Confession of Faith in the Kupu Whakapono affirms ethnic unity and diversity, and since its BOO provides guidelines that encourage consultative relations between distinct groups, these relations would be found at the congregational level as well. But since the BOO has nothing to say about such relations at the local level, does this suggest that ethnic unity and diversity is not so obvious, or perhaps even absent in local congregations?

Conclusion

This is the vital question: How is this rich theological imperative which we have examined, and which is so clearly intimated at the global, national, and regional levels of the PCANZ, worked out on the ground in the lived experience of congregational life and ministry? It raises other important questions as well. Do congregations of the PCANZ organise themselves according to the ecclesiology they believe and confess, or according to the ethnic and cultural preferences of their members? Do they reflect the diversity of the Church or are they inclined to be ethnically homogeneous? Perhaps it should also be asked whether or not the PCANZ policy of diversity determines what should be done at the local level. In other words, should PCANZ congregations be ethnically diverse simply because the national body confesses it? And if diversity is not found at the local level, does it mean that congregations and the national Church are failing in this respect?

These are pressing questions and, for me, personal ones born out of my own experiences of church ministry within the PCANZ. I have served in congregations whose membership happily affirmed their Christian identity and unity, although they tended to demonstrate it in ethnically and culturally specific ways. Similarly, exploring a Christological and Trinitarian ecclesiology has been significant because this is what the PCANZ considers itself to uphold. But does it, in practice, do so at the local level?

I believe that part of the answer to these questions also lies in understanding the development of the four main ethnic components of the PCANZ. This will give some historical context to why PCANZ congregations are the way they are today. We examine that next.

3 – Historical Development of PCANZ Ethnic Components

Ethnicity has a significant influence upon the way people relate with others. It can sway how people organise their community life, particularly in ways that affirm ethnic and cultural similarity. Previously, we noted the view that ethnocentric tendencies within religious communities of the American context were possibly a result of historical roots of racism and discriminatory practices that alienated minority groups. In this chapter I examine the historical development of Presbyterianism in New Zealand among the four main ethnic components of the PCANZ: European, Māori, Asian and Pacific Islander. This exploration will assist us to identify whether the same ethnocentric trends are also evident in their development. If so, it will be interesting to see how deeply entrenched these tendencies are, and how they shape the congregations within the various components. Part of the exploration of Presbyterianism will include the influence of cultural agency that might also have a bearing upon the religio-cultural identity of these components. The results will provide insights for the way we understand the nature of PCANZ congregations today.

Development of the European Component

Presbyterianism was introduced to New Zealand mainly through the Church of Scotland in 1840 and the Free Church of Scotland in 1848. Later, there were also Presbyterian strands from England and Ireland, as well as a mix of clergy from other European denominations. Although it had a strong Scottish heritage, it was very much a European church in its Reformation roots.

The arrival of Presbyterians in New Zealand was a response to religious and economic tensions in Scotland. The Church of Scotland felt increasing discontent amongst its leaders with regard to its own church government, leading to the Disruption of 1843.[152] Scottish society in general experienced growing poverty and displacement of its citizens, whereby those financially devastated from other places crammed into the slums of its industrial cities, with their sub-standard living conditions.[153] Those who decided to leave such a troubled environment by migrating to New Zealand did so with the hope of a better life for themselves as individuals, as a people, and as a Church. In many ways this migration "provided a chance for a new beginning to re-establish all that was noble of Scottish religion and culture."[154]

Despite the internal conflicts of Presbyterianism in Scotland, there was a clear intention that the church to be transplanted in the new land should reflect, as far as possible, the ideal religious and cultural values of the homeland church. Scottish Presbyterians took with them a great sense of pride regarding who they were and what they represented. John Dickson describes the ethnocentric spirit of those leaving their shores in 1840:

> "Every inch of their native land was dear to them … There was no land in the world, in their estimation, so beautiful as their native land, no religion so Scriptural as the Presbyterian religion, and no people so free, so enlightened, so homely, and so dear unto them, as the Scottish people – the relations, the friends and countrymen among whom they had been brought up."[155]

Presbyterians arrived in New Zealand some 30 years after the (Anglican) Church Missionary Society (CMS) and the (Methodist) Wesleyan Missionary Society (WMS). With the thrust of Western colonialism and missionary endeavours from Europe into other parts of the world, Presbyterians came with the vision of expanding European Presbyterian communities throughout New Zealand. Presbyterianism was thus established not as a missionary movement among Māori, but as a European settler faith.[156]

Emigrating overseas was not considered by most early European Presbyterians as temporary; rather, it was an intentional process to plant and nurture their own people in order to create a new society in a new land. Clergy who accompanied settlers on the journey were seen as part of a "systematic provision of minister and church."[157] As an ethnically homogeneous immigrant group they were a European church transplanted by Europeans, for Europeans, and led by Europeans in a new country. Their hope was that "the day would come when the Church of Scotland should have in New Zealand more churches than she could number in the motherland."[158] This suggests that the Presbyterian Church in New Zealand would not only reflect better numbers than those in the homeland, but more importantly, the kinds of people in these churches – Presbyterians of European heritage.

By establishing congregations within European settlements, towns or cities around New Zealand, the Presbyterian Church also sought to reflect its European roots. For example, it incorporated its traditions such as the Kirk Session, Deacon's Court, Presbyteries and General Assembly. The erection of its church buildings until relatively recent times demonstrated a sense of European "sophistication and capability that was considered a catalyst of and precondition for all progress in civilisation."[159] Although the Presbyterian Church had an opportunity to redefine itself in a new country, it understandably still held onto its roots that made it what it was – a European child born in the image of its European parent.

For much of its early history, up until the inclusion of non-Europeans, the PCANZ was very much European in outlook and organisation. Apart from a few who committed themselves to working amongst Māori, Asians and Pacific Islanders, the majority of European Presbyterians remained in ministries and congregations that were predominantly, if not totally, European. From 1840 to 1901, 411 ministers had served in Presbyterian ministries.[160] All of them were European. From 1902 to the end of 1940 a further 504 ministers served in the Church. Of this number, only two were non-European. One was William Yau Chan, who was ordained in 1904 and who served the Chinese church in Dunedin; the other was Timutimu Tioke, a Māori, who was ordained by the General Assembly in 1931 to serve in the Māori Missions.[161] Within the Dunedin presbytery from 1947 to 1991, a total of 213 served as ministers and lay leaders of parishes within its bounds. All but nine were European.[162] Clearly, PCANZ congregations were almost entirely homogeneous.

Some European ministers served in non-European missions and ministries but, by and large, European church leadership was reserved for ministry amongst predominantly European congregations. In some cases the homogeneous nature of this relationship was to help meet religious, ethnic and cultural needs. For example, the experience of Dutch immigrants in congregations within the presbytery of Auckland saw a Dutch minister, Rev. W. Van Wyngen, appointed by the New Settlers' Committee. Van Wyngen had oversight of all Presbyterian Dutch colonists throughout New Zealand. The chief intention of the committee was to integrate the newcomers into the life of existing European congregations. According to Horace Crawford, the challenges for such a task "led the Church to realise that extra Dutch ministers were needed and that, as a temporary measure at least, the folk from Holland should have personal oversight by pastors of their own."[163] As well as ministers, the Netherlands Reformed Church also sent elders, managers, organists, Bible Class leaders and Sunday School teachers to assist the Dutch ministry in the Presbyterian Church.[164] This is an instance of an early pan-ethnic dynamic within the European component. Although integration sought to unify European nationalities, the particular ethnic and cultural needs or preferences of particular groups made distinctions between them more marked.

When European congregations did have the opportunity to integrate with non-European groups who joined them, the relationship was not always easy. We will return to this later in the chapter, but it is worth noting in this section some of the implications for the European component of the PCANZ. The official merger of the Congregational Church of New Zealand and the Presbyterian Church of New Zealand in 1969 involved the mass joining of Pacific Islander congregations and ministers. This proved to be significant for some congregations.

For example, at First Church of Otago in Dunedin (founded in 1848), the inclusion of Pacific Islander members (mainly Samoans) from the Moray Place Congregational Church as early as 1966 provoked a marked transition from being an all-European congregation to one that was ethnically diverse.[165] It is not clear whether this move was an attempt to alter the pattern of ethnic homogeneity in the church, but the relationship was clearly a "steep learning curve" for First Church and Presbyterianism in general.[166] Although the relationship began with genuine enthusiasm for unity in its first few years, European and Samoan members of the congregation began to have "inter-racial problems" over language and cultural practices.[167] As a result of increasing tensions, there was some evidence of "white flight," in which prominent families moved to other predominantly European churches and a substantial number of Samoans in Dunedin left to form their own congregation in the north end of the city.[168] The membership of First Church is still ethnically diverse today, despite its long history of homogeneity. But the fact that many have left to be part of other congregations in which they share the same ethnicity demonstrates a strong desire for ethnic and cultural independence.

Development of the Māori Component

In the first 50 years of Presbyterianism in New Zealand, Presbyterian work among Māori was very limited. Apart from the initial efforts of James Duncan in 1843, Māori missions were implemented on behalf of the Presbyterian Church by German Lutherans Johann Riemenschneider, Abraham Honoré, and J. F. H. Wohlers, and by Māori Methodist missionary Patoromu Pu.[169] By the end of the 1800s (when Henry Fletcher began his work among Māori, which would later prove significant) the Church "was far from enthusiastic about its Māori work" and "her earlier efforts had well-nigh petered out."[170]

The lack of interest in Māori by European Presbyterians was reciprocated by Māori. This was reflected in the lack of Māori numbers in the Church. This may partly be attributed to various factors such as the growing mistrust by Māori of the Christian church (especially European clergy), in light of the dishonouring of the Treaty of Waitangi, land confiscations, the increasing population and domination of Europeans and European culture in New Zealand, and the rise of religious Māori groups such as the Ringatu and Ratana Churches.[171] In the main, however, Māori remained resistant to Presbyterianism because it was "a faith which seemed to them austere, over-intellectual, and far too condemnatory of their way of life."[172] Since Presbyterianism was a European settler faith, any involvement Māori had with it was marked by caution, wherein they kept their distance.

Māori eventually became part of the Presbyterian Church, but their participation was shaped in a way that encouraged homogeneous development. As the predominantly European Presbyterian Church sought to develop its interests nationally and internationally (in overseas missions), it left Māori ministry to develop on its own, without much support. The Presbyterian Church's relationship with Māori was exemplified by the geographical confinement of Māori missions and pastorates to the Tuhoe region and neighbouring areas in the North Island. Most Māori involved with these pastorates have a strong identification with Tuhoe.

The reluctance to pursue a wider geographical scope of work among Māori may be due to the fact that Presbyterians did not want to compete with the extensive national missionary efforts of the CMS and WMS. However, it could also be seen as a cultural, geographical, and perhaps relational divide between Māori and non-Māori Presbyterians. The Tuhoe region was an area known as the "cradle of Māori pacifism, nationalism and resistance to assimilation" due to Māori religio-political figures of the Ringatu faith such as Te Kooti and Rua Kēnana, who reserved their activities mainly within the Urewera area.[173] Tuhoe chiefs were not signatories to the Treaty of Waitangi; and with ongoing struggles of land confiscation, the strong following by Māori of figures like Te Kooti and Rua Kēnana was a challenge to Presbyterian missions. The salient point for our interests is that the confinement of Presbyterian ministry to such an area and people clearly encouraged a homogeneous development within the Māori component of the Church.

The lack of interest among Māori in the predominantly European church did not mean a total lack of their interest in the Māori component of the Presbyterian Church. This was in part due to the extremely effective ways in which European deaconesses worked within Māori settlements, particularly with children, eventually leading to the establishment of schools for Māori children.[174] According to Lachy Paterson, Presbyterian missions among Māori "would not have been able to operate had it not been for their efforts."[175] At the same time, the work of John G. Laughton since 1918 at Maungapohatu, the stronghold of Rua Kēnana, eventually proved pivotal for the growing receptivity of Presbyterianism by Māori. Despite not totally agreeing with all aspects of Kēnana's religious beliefs and practices, Laughton and Kēnana developed a close friendship that enabled better ties between the two faith communities.[176]

Towards the middle of the 20th century, numerous reports to General Assemblies on the ongoing struggles of staff shortages and lack of resources for Māori missions highlighted the wide gulf that existed between Māori and the rest of the Church. It was a time of changing perceptions of Māori about themselves in the Church. According to James Irwin, it was a time to throw off the image of Māori missions as "Cinderella, neglected and passed over."[177] The image here of Māori life in the Presbyterian Church family is one of disconnection and disadvantage.

However, as the Māori population began making a resurgence, so too did their aspirations for self-determination and a Māori expression of Christian faith within the life of the Church.[178] This led to the disestablishment of the Māori Missions Committee and the inception of Te Hinota Māori (Māori Synod) in 1954, now known as Te Aka Puaho. As a long-serving minister in Māori missions and a primary catalyst for the move toward greater Māori autonomy in the Church, Laughton argued that it was imperative for Māori to recapture their own culture and to consolidate the things that were the very essence of their life. Autonomy for Māori was not to be seen as creating isolation or separation from the rest of the Church; rather, it was a means of recognising equal partnership as a principle consistent with *tino rangatiratanga* – self-determination.

> The Māoris being a minority race scattered throughout the land in which the Pakeha people predominate are groping for the very survival of their own very distinctive life and for its satisfaction… No individual can develop in a situation in which he is repressed, and this is precisely the unhappy fate of the Māori when he is denied the society of his own people, without which he cannot be himself or find the things for which he craves. He can work the better and the happier in co-operation in the world of the Pakeha if he has the security of his heritage. It is there in the atmosphere which is home to his spirit that his true self expression is attained and the unhampered development of his personality takes place.[179]

In essence, Laughton's statement promoted the idea that Māori ministry would be better served through culturally relevant ways by Māori themselves. Although he did not advocate segregation between Māori and non-Māori, Laughton encouraged having the space, opportunity, and freedom for Māori to develop themselves in ways that affirmed their ethnic, cultural, and religious identity, without interference from non-Māori. This view may have enhanced relations between Māori and Presbyterianism. A sense of Māori autonomy in the Presbyterian Church perhaps encouraged Kēnana, on his deathbed, to ask Laughton to "take care of my children."[180] Kēnana's children would be the future of the Māori component of the PCANZ.

The appeal of Māori homogeneity reflected their religious connections. Tuhoe Māori had links with the Māori component of the Presbyterian Church, yet they also equally allied themselves with the Ratana and Ringatu Churches which consisted totally of Māori under Māori leadership. The common denominator for Māori involvement was that these were perceived as Māori churches that affirmed both Māori identity as well as the Christian faith. The important unit that defines Māori is the tribe and not, as it was for Europeans, the nuclear family.[181] Māori, therefore, found their true sense of identity and belonging through wider connections among their own kind. The Ratana and Ringatu Churches were embraced by Māori not only because they were represented by Māori, but also because many actually had family connections with them.[182] It was not uncommon for Māori to be involved with a number of these churches despite being an official member of only one of them. What seems more important were the ethnic, cultural, and familial ties that affirmed Māori homogeneity.

The strong cultural value of community permeated every area of Māori life, from its relationship to the land to the way it saw its history and future. Although mission stations were gradually set up in different places as centres for ministry among Māori, ministry with Māori occurred at their *pa* (fortified village) or places of temporary residence during periods of travel.[183] Unlike the situation in some Pacific islands, where the islander converts resided at the mission station, Māori remained on their own land among their own people rather than mixing and living with European missionaries.

For Māori the land was their *turangawaewae* – a place of standing. Turangawaewae is a fundamental concept in Māori life. It does not represent mere ownership of a piece of land. For Māori, their whole history and cultural heritage is enshrined in their tribal land, in which they have a share, of which they feel themselves to be a part, and which gives them the right of participation in the community life of their people.[184]

This did not mean that Māori never engaged with others in European settlements or never participated in activities at the mission stations. But the special connection they had with their land meant that they were more inclined to have most religious activities performed at places holding spiritual significance for them. This was understandable considering their frustration and ill-feeling at the loss of most of their land by the coercive means and greed of European colonialism. Yet the consequence of geographic isolation also meant isolation from fellowship with most non-Māori.

The sense of "separateness" between Māori and non-Māori was also evident when attempts were made to bring them together. For example, although Taupo was a dual pastorate to Māori and European alike, the worship services and church work by the two groups were very much separate: "The Māori services were conducted in the Māori settlements, and in the Māori language, those more specifically for the European community were held in the Pakeha settlements, and in the English language. Very few Māori attended any of the English language services in spite of the fact that one minister served both races."[185] By 1953 the huge growth of the European population in Taupo also saw an increase in the European membership and adherents of the combined Māori and European congregation. This led to the move by the European part of the church to become a separate congregation.[186] Similar experiences were seen in the Taumarunui and Kawerau pastorates.

The development of Māori Christian communities also included the development of Māori leaders, particularly clergy. It took nearly 91 years after the arrival of Presbyterianism before the first Māori minister, Timutimu Tioke, was ordained in 1931. This was in spite of the fact that Presbyterian Māori missions were greatly indebted to indigenous converts who, as Raeburn Lange rightly points out, "played a decisive role" in the spread of Christianity among Māori.[187]

Although a growing number of European clergy and deaconesses eventually established themselves in ministry among Māori, the importance and need for Māori church leadership became increasingly apparent. Māori clergy represented Māori leadership in both church and community. Having tribal and familial ties to Māori communities enabled Māori clergy to gain greater acceptance and influence in many areas of Māori life. For example, Hemi Potatau's long service in Taumarunui, up to 1959, after returning from duty in the armed forces, enabled a very strong foundation for growth among his own people.[188]

The need for more Māori clergy in Māori ministry brought to the fore the issue of ministry training. The establishment of the Māori Synod was recognition that the future of Christianity among Māori lay in developing strong indigenous leaders.[189] This prompted the discussion and then fulfilment in 1954 of the establishment of a Māori school of ministry training called "Te Wananga A Rangi" in Whakatane.[190] This was an institution primarily, though not exclusively, designed for Māori students. Instead of Māori training at an unfamiliar place and in the unaccustomed climate and culture of the Knox Theological Hall in Dunedin, they could train at Whakatane in a setting relevant to Māori ministry, without separating the students from their home environment.[191] A past Moderator of Te Aka Puaho, Wayne Tekaawa, comments on the contrasting experiences of Māori ministry students within the two institutions:

> They were trained in their own environment amongst their own people; their language was the accepted medium of communication, teaching and expression while the curriculum reflected their situation where they could study their own church history and pastoral and theological practices; equipping them for lifelong ministry to their own people. As opposed to coming to the Theological Hall where they looked different, the language was not their language and they struggled to express themselves in their own acceptable ways and you were trained to minister or fit [into] another context when others around them could stay in their familiar comfort zones.[192]

The incorporation and development of non-stipendiary ministers – *minita amorangi* – was a response to the growing vacancies among Māori congregations and the lack of students training for ordained ministry. The term *Amorangi* has its roots deep within Māori spiritualism and its definition, elaboration and expression are as different as is the theology that informs them.[193] Amorangi ministry is one firmly grounded within and inextricably connected to its Māori community. In contrast to nationally ordained ministry within the PCANZ where a minister can be called to serve in any congregation anywhere in New Zealand, Tekaawa posits that

> Amorangi ministry challenges that somewhat in that while you may belong to Christ, you first and foremost belong to your Iwi… Instead of attending a seminary for study formation and reflection the locus of your studies is in the community that you come from; you are never separated from your people … You are born into your Iwi, it is your Iwi who must support your call to ministry alongside your local parish, in fact it would be fair to say that your Iwi is your local Church and not a separate or different community of individual believers within a wider community who gather on a Sunday… the Church is the glue that holds your Iwi together … In many ways Amorangi arises from the people, to the people, for the people.[194]

There is definitely a strong Māori cultural identity that permeates the life of Christian communities within Te Aka Puaho. This is particularly evident in its church leadership and culturally relevant model of ministry that it hopes to carry out amongst its own people. In this respect, the developing ministry of Te Aka Puaho is clearly Māori-focused, grounded in the desire and need for an authentic Māori Christian expression.

Development of the Asian Component

Presbyterian work among Asians in New Zealand has been ongoing for nearly a hundred and fifty years. It began with initiatives by Europeans from Knox Church in Dunedin that saw the Synod of Otago and Southland establish a mission to the Chinese who flocked to the area during the gold rush era of the mid-1800s.[195] Although initiated by Europeans, from the outset it was considered strategically and culturally effective to have a Chinese Christian serving in mission among Chinese miners. In 1870 a Methodist-trained catechist from Victoria, Australia, Paul (Wan) Ah Chin, was appointed to work among the Cantonese-speaking Chinese in the gold fields of Lawrence and Tuapeka.[196]

Despite being more fluent in Mandarin than Cantonese, the ethnic and cultural similarity between Chin and the largely Cantonese-speaking Chinese communities enabled his ministry to be very successful. After only a year of ministry the group of Chinese who regularly attended his church meetings ranged from fifteen to twenty.[197] The growth of Chin's ministry meant that a larger venue was required for their religious meetings.[198] Furthermore, it led to Chinese converts encouraging growing numbers of Chinese to attend religious meetings and thereby helped consolidate Chinese communities that were often geographically scattered.[199] There was no doubt in the mind of the Church that Chin's ethnic and cultural compatibility with his fellow Chinese "proved himself to be in the best measure fitted for his arduous work and his labours have been crowned with a fair measure of success."[200] In many respects, Chin's achievement among Chinese on New Zealand soil reflected much of the effectiveness of Asian Christian converts in early Christian missions in places like China and Korea.[201]

However, it might be asked whether the same success could be achieved by a non-Chinese person. After Chin's departure, Rev. Hugh Cowie, who had seventeen years' experience serving in China, began working among those previously ministered to by Chin. Due to ill health, and particularly because he lacked command of the Cantonese language, Cowie lasted only about eight months in his ministry.[202] Considering the effectiveness of Paul Ah Chin and the short-term failure of Hugh Cowie, appointing another Chinese worker seemed an obvious choice. Yet for reasons unknown, the next to champion Presbyterianism among Chinese in New Zealand was another European minister, Alexander Don.

Don began his work in 1881 having had a relatively limited experience in the mission fields of Canton, China, in 1879. Even with a Chinese teacher who accompanied him back to New Zealand, Don's grasp of Cantonese language and culture was "elementary" at best.[203]

Although Don's physical stamina and determination were outstanding compared to Cowie, the many accounts of his inland tours among the Chinese of Central Otago conveyed the same disappointments that Cowie experienced. This was in part due to the harsh terrain and weather conditions he endured in Central Otago, but perhaps more so to the great reluctance of Chinese to engage with and accept him in any significant way. Don's frustration early in his work convinced him that only a Chinese Christian would have a better showing in the mission effort:

> Many times when passing them I have said, 'Preaching of Jesus to-day; please come and hear,' but the invitation has never to my knowledge had any direct effect … It is in positions like these that the Chinese catechist, with his immensely superior knowledge of the Chinese mind, would be invaluable.[204]

In Don's mind, ethnic and cultural relevance in the relationship between church worker and Chinese was imperative for successful ministry. This did not mean that Don's efforts were total failures, but he clearly conceded that the task of meaningful religious engagement was much harder and came at a greater cost for those who were ethnically and culturally different.

At this point it is also important to acknowledge that Don's work among the Chinese was not a solo effort. Like Paul Ah Chin's experiences, the service of Chinese co-workers is worth noting. Timothy Fay Loie, a Chinese Christian from the Dunedin mission, was one who continued the inland tours for two years during the absence of Don.[205] Others helpful to the Chinese mission were the few and scattered Chinese converts who continued to reside in the goldfields.[206] These Chinese converts were not only vital as guides for Don in locating Chinese, but also instrumental for the promotion of religious meetings and encouraging fellow Chinese to attend them.[207] Such men were influential in conducting group discussions or debates among other Chinese about the Christian faith. These Chinese Christians opened doors of opportunity to engage more effectively with their fellow country-folk in ways that non-Chinese like Don could not.

By 1911 the Chinese population in New Zealand had dramatically dwindled due to the lack of gold found, as well as the Poll Tax imposed upon Chinese immigrants. Many Chinese returned home or moved elsewhere and entered into new areas of work in towns and cities. As a response to this development, the Foreign Missions Office of the Presbyterian Church increased the number of Chinese Christian workers in the New Zealand Chinese missions.[208] The move from Chinese mission centres to the establishment of Chinese churches continued to highlight the peculiar relationship of Chinese with their Christian leaders. Of interest is how this was reflected when a Chinese and non-Chinese minister or leader was in charge. For instance, the Annual Reports of 1905, 1907 and 1909 for the Chinese Church in Dunedin show that when Rev. Don, as the minister of the church, was away on his mission tours, Rev. William Chan, Mr. Timothy Loie, and Mr. F. L. Law would be responsible for ministry. During these periods, lasting between two to three months at times, the Church experienced dramatic increases in Chinese Christians attending worship services and Christian education classes for children.[209] Susan Irvine particularly noted that the work of Mr. Law in the periods 1909-1910 and 1926-1931 "brought new enthusiasm. In these years the Church was again a centre for Dunedin Chinese people."[210] Conversely, when a European minister, Andrew L. Miller (considered a thoroughly competent missionary with a quick understanding of the Cantonese language and psychology), was appointed in February 1939, his first Annual Report noted the decrease in the attendance of Chinese in worship services and Sunday school.[211] Again, we see here the effects of the ethno-cultural match and mismatch between clergy and congregation.

Although much of early Presbyterian history among Asians in New Zealand is focused on the Chinese, the 1980s saw the inclusion of other Asian nationalities into the life of the Church. This was mainly due to the immigration policy changes of 1987 that enabled large numbers of migrants arriving from different parts of Asia.[212] These groups of Asian Christians quickly transitioned from informal religious gatherings to established PCANZ congregations in their own right. From 1987 to 1995, Indonesian, Taiwanese and Korean congregations were planted in the Auckland region.[213] Although there are pockets of Asian people in various predominantly non-Asian congregations, the majority fellowship amongst their own people.

As a response to the emergence of Asian congregations and the need to provide appropriate ministry, the Committee for Development of Asian Ministries was formed in 1993.[214] This committee sought continually to bring Asian ministry concerns to the PCANZ and to help develop national strategies to enable Asian congregations to access the various governing bodies within the Church. The challenge for Asian groups was that most wanted to join Presbyterian congregations but, at the same time, remain relatively autonomous in the way they organised themselves. For Koreans in particular, although they may come from Presbyterian churches in Korea, these are churches that lean more towards a congregational polity as opposed to a conciliar one lived out by the PCANZ. To assist them, the minister or "Evangelist" was an important role, not only for initiating and caring for such groups, but also for their transition and development into full membership with the PCANZ.[215] They were usually ministers from overseas churches that represented the faith and ethnic/cultural traditions of the particular Asian group.[216] It was very rare for Asian congregations to have a minister or leader who was not of the same ethnicity and culture as the congregation. Although some Asian congregations have had European ministers working with them, the huge disproportion between Asian and non-Asian ministers within Asian congregations suggests their preference for Asian ministers. Similar to what we saw with Chinese congregations, the homogeneous dynamic also developed amongst other Asian congregations.

The move to consolidate as Asian congregations was also paralleled amongst its own ministers. In 2000 the Committee for the Development of Asian Ministries became the Council of Asian Congregations. Although representation of the Council is Pan-Asian, there is a sub-group of the Korean Ministers' Association.[217] Moreover, most Asian ministers serving in the PCANZ have come from overseas churches.[218] The endorsement of the call to accept them is testament to the understanding of the PCANZ that its Asian congregations are better served by ministers who are ethnically and culturally compatible. This may also have been necessary due to the lack of appropriate personnel and resources through its own systems to meet the ministry needs of its Asian members. Perhaps it reflects, as well, the cultural limitations that non-Asian ministers have in working amongst Asian parishioners. Despite the valuable contributions that non-Asian ministers have made to ministry within Asian congregations, their growing numbers seem indicative of the preference for an ethnically homogeneous dynamic.

While joining the PCANZ can be seen as a sign of the willingness of Asians to integrate into the wider life of the Church, Asian congregations and ministers have remained somewhat detached from most non-Asian congregations in the PCANZ. The majority engage and participate when they have to in the corporate matters of the Church, but by and large they confine themselves to matters more relevant to the religio-cultural needs of their own contexts. Being on the fringes has been a sign of some congregations not totally fitting in with the Presbyterian ethos and systems of operation.[219] Some have come from traditions that are more Congregational than Presbyterian in ethos, which has implications for the way they organise themselves and participate within the PCANZ.[220]

Although Asians can be found in other congregations (usually and largely European), the reality for most, according to Stuart Vogel, is that "Asian congregations and language specific ministries continue to form and respond to the needs of their migrant cohorts in culturally familiar ways."[221] Even though some non-Asian congregations may initially play host to groups of migrant Christians who are trying to make a home for themselves in the PCANZ, Vogel moreover states that "many English-speaking congregations fail to hold the Asian or Pacific members. In some congregations, different ethnic groups merely co-exist side by side and politely ignore each other. In other cases, 'white flight' takes place as Asian and/or Pacific Island numbers grow and European members go elsewhere."[222]

Generally speaking, there is the deeper concern that Asian congregations still struggle with a sense of belonging within the PCANZ. This may be due to ethnic, cultural and ecclesiological differences at various levels in the church. But even within the Asian component, there has been little mixing of specific Asian groups. Unlike the situation of pan-Asian churches identified in the United States, within the PCANZ there has not been any such development.

There seems to be a preference for each Asian nationality to evolve in ways that are ethnic/cultural-specific. Overall, ethnocentrism has been evident in the development of Asian ministries.

Development Of The Pacific Islander Component

Christian ministry amongst Pacific Islanders in New Zealand commenced through the Congregational Union of New Zealand (CUNZ) as early as the 1940s.[223] Unlike the mission status given to work among Māori and Chinese in New Zealand, Pacific Islanders arriving from their homelands with church backgrounds were incorporated into churches without much difficulty.[224] Those who came from Protestant and Catholic traditions in the homeland naturally joined those churches when arriving in New Zealand.

Ministry to Pacific Islanders in the PCANZ has its roots in the reception of a significant portion of the CUNZ into the PCANZ in 1969.[225] This saw the majority of ministers and congregations, including the entire Pacific Islanders branch of the CUNZ, being incorporated. One of the conditions of joining the PCANZ was that "the organisational basis of the Pacific Islanders' Church should be preserved."[226] Therefore, from its beginning in the PCANZ, the relationship of the distinctive Pacific Islanders' component with the rest of the Church was clearly recognised. To appreciate the development of the Pacific Islanders' component, it is most helpful to consider its history from within the CUNZ and its continuance into the PCANZ. Both contexts will assist in identifying how ethnic and cultural issues have influenced its growth.

In its formative years the Pacific Islanders' component was largely an immigrant church. It began through informal gatherings in homes, garages or school halls for respective island groups of Samoans, Cook Islanders and Niueans. In their different fellowships, each group was able to conduct its religious affairs in ways relevant to its own cultural background. The language, traditions, and identity of each island group were clearly distinct and reaffirmed in these religious enclaves. The religious gatherings of Pacific Christians early in their history were ethnically homogeneous, where their practices were those that they brought from their respective island homes. This allowed them to gain familiarity and solidarity in a new country and culture. The ethnic-specific nature of these Pacific groups shaped their identity as they began their journey in the church in New Zealand.

Ministry to Pacific peoples by the likes of Rev Robert Challis eventually brought together the different island groups under his pastoral care. In the 1940s, a small group of Cook Islanders attended the Beresford Street Congregational Church in Auckland.[227] Gradually, small but increasing numbers of Samoans and Niueans were incorporated into the fellowship. This shifted Pacific Christians from their respective homogeneous gatherings into a collective body that saw the birth and development of the Pacific Islanders' Congregational Church (PICC) in 1947.[228] They may have been a Pacific Islander congregation in a generic sense, but more pan-Pacific in actuality.

The Beresford Street church at the time already had a European congregation which, to some extent, welcomed the inclusion of their Pacific Christian neighbours. This created a new dynamic of diversity, but with its challenges. In terms of communication, Pacific people generally struggled with the English language. According to Challis:

> When the islanders came here first they went to our churches with some hesitation. Few went regularly, because although they could manage daily life and work with a limited understanding of English, they found 'religious English' beyond them. One New Zealand church order decided to found a church for island people. Here the people could worship in their own tongues and in the ways to which they had become accustomed.[229]

Having a separate church for Pacific Islanders to accommodate their religio-cultural needs was a positive step forward, but it also indicated that ethnic diversity in the church was much more difficult to sustain.

Although Pacific Islanders had their own church building, the same challenges of diversity amongst the respective island groups followed them. What language and practices would they adopt as a collective of Pacific peoples in their own church? Having their own language expressed in the church context was very important for first-generation Pacific immigrants in that church became a "temporary retirement from the stresses and strains of everyday life."[230] Although there were combined worship services for all island groups to attend, the appeal of the vernacular in the context of worship saw the respective groups also establish separate worship services incorporating their own language and cultural protocols. This further affirmed and promoted each island identity.

The value of Pacific culture and the Christian faith led Pacific Islander churches to find other ways of encouraging the cultural and religious needs of the respective island groups. One way was to allow each group to have use of the church premises on allocated evenings for developing their own fellowship. Although this was helpful in providing space for strengthening the spiritual and cultural aspirations of each island group, it also created a sense of separation between them. The challenge was balancing support for and loyalty to the interests of the congregation as a whole while doing the same for the respective island groups. Pacific Islanders may have valued their different island relationships with each other and with Europeans and adopted English as a common language to facilitate those relations, but they increasingly found it appealing to participate within their own cultural arena for religious purposes.

As the Pacific population began to grow in New Zealand, through increasing immigration, so too did Pacific congregations. They spread from Auckland in the north to Invercargill in the south. The growth reflected a greater sense of solidarity and ecclesiastical strength for the Pacific Islanders' component. At the local level, the size of island groups within various congregations also mirrored their ethnic and cultural strength.[231] Apart from the immigration factor, the growth of Samoan groups may have also been influenced by the intimate correlation that exists between the *fa'asamoa* (Samoan culture) and the church, whereby Samoan culture is very much reflected in church culture.[232]

When numerical strength of a particular group facilitates a greater expression of its own spiritual and cultural identity, it can also engender a spirit of independence. An example of this is demonstrated in the Samoan members of the New Lynn congregation. After expressing their desire for worship services in their language, they eventually left to establish a totally separate Samoan church.[233] This clearly shows how ethnocentrism can feed homogeneity and separatism. In terms of the stress for the vernacular to be used in worship, Betty Duncan noted that prayers became religiously authentic for Samoan-speaking elders only when conducted in their mother tongue: "Worship in English had little meaning for those who could not understand it, and this generated feelings of alienation when language separated a person from his or her church traditions and teachings."[234] In this case it was important for the Samoan group at New Lynn to be on their own so that they would not compromise their cultural and religious values by being integrated with non-Samoan groups in the church. But it also shows that such a move reflected a narrow homogeneous and theological view that could not extend beyond ethnic and cultural boundaries to make Christian unity in diversity work.

The assertiveness of Pacific identity in the church was also reflected in its leadership. Decades of rapid growth saw not only new branches appear throughout the country, but also increasing numbers of Pacific clergy. Some clergy, such as Rev. Tariu Teaia, a Cook Islander, were initially brought into New Zealand from the island churches to cater for the needs of their people.[235] However, many were later trained in theological institutions in New Zealand and ordained within New Zealand parishes. By 1967 there were eleven full-time Pacific Islander ministers within the PICC, and by 1969 there were twenty congregations established around the country.[236]

The inclusion and increase of Pacific clergy played a significant part in the development of Pacific Islander congregations. Considering the high status that Pacific Islanders generally gave to ministers and the influence that ministers were able to exert given that status, it made sense to encourage the training and appointment of Pacific clergy. Although lay leadership was an integral component of Pacific Islander congregations, the introduction and development of islander clergy further consolidated the religious and cultural status of these congregations. This was not a sign of disrespect or lack of appreciation for the services of non-Pacific Islander ministers to Pacific Islander congregations. Having ministers who shared the same ethnicity and culture as that of an island group within the congregation seemed to affirm the ministry as well as the relationship. Again, this ethnically parallel relationship mirrored those from the earlier history of Christian missions in their Pacific homelands, where much of the evangelism and establishment of Christian churches was largely enabled by islander converts.[237] For example, although Rev. Challis commanded huge respect among Samoans, Cook Islanders and Niueans within the congregation of the Auckland church, Rev. Leuatea Sio, a Samoan who was appointed in 1957 as an assistant to Rev Challis, was regarded by the Samoan part of the congregation as "a leader who personified the ideal marriage to Samoans of its tradition and the church."[238] Sio's leadership in the church became increasingly prevalent among the Samoan group, while Challis' leadership was mainly reserved for the Cook Islanders and Niueans.

Eventually the growing desire to cater for the religio-cultural needs of Cook Islanders and Niueans saw the appointments of Rev. Teura Lucky Mave, a Cook Islander, in 1966, and Rev. Lagaua Talagi, a Niuean, in 1971.[239] Now the Pacific Islanders' Church in Auckland had ministers whose ethnicity and culture matched the respective island groups within it. Although all ministers were accepted and respected as ministers for the whole church, their roles increasingly became focused within a particular ethnic group. Similarities were also seen in the development of the Pacific Islanders' Church in Newtown, Wellington.

Although the early model of PIC churches was pan-Pacific in nature, the increasing sense of identity and independence within island groups led to their establishing themselves on their own. The term "PIC" was generic for a mix of Pacific peoples in a congregation. However, from the time when the New Lynn Samoan group became the Glen Eden PIC, the term has become more of a general identification with the Pacific component of the PCANZ, while particular congregations could in fact remain ethnic-specific in representation.

Some congregations have kept the term "PIC" in their name while also including the ethnic group they represent: for example, "Manukau PIC (Samoan)" and "Invercargill PIC (Samoan)."[240] Others have dropped the term PIC altogether and have identified themselves in terms of their specific ethnicity and location; for example, "Invercargill Cook Islands Presbyterian Church," "Cook

Islanders Presbyterian Church (Wellington Region)," Manukau Cook Islanders' Presbyterian Parish" and "Samoan Presbyterian Church Onehunga."[241] Some congregations that share church premises also retain their ethnic identity in their name; for example, "Avondale Union Parish (Samoan Speaking Fellowship)" in Auckland, and "St. James' Presbyterian (Niuean)" and "St. James' Presbyterian (English)" in Wellington.[242] Although "PIC" is a term and concept that tries to encapsulate the religious association of Pacific peoples in the PCANZ, island groups are increasingly choosing to establish themselves in ways that specifically express their cultural identity as distinct from other island groups.

The Pacific Islanders' component appears to have had a very distinctive life before and after its inclusion into the PCANZ. Although non-Pacific peoples were part of its development in its very early years, it has increasingly become homogeneous in terms of the particularity of island groups and clergy represented in its congregations. In short, ethnocentric tendencies appear to have influenced the Pacific Islanders' component to a large degree.

Cultural Agency

The development of Presbyterianism in New Zealand highlights the cultural identity of the four main ethnic components of the PCANZ. Congregations of these components reflect a largely homogeneous character that appears to be a result of entrenched ethnocentrism. This raises the issue of cultural agency: who is primarily responsible for religio-cultural change in these communities? Is it those presenting the gospel from the outside or those receiving it from the inside? Moreover, how is it done?

It is undeniable that the introduction of Presbyterianism into New Zealand was also an introduction of European culture. The Christian traditions that Presbyterians brought to New Zealand were culturally laden. The link between colonialism and the expansion of Christian missions is summed up by Jehu Hanciles: "The Western missionary project not only derived considerable impetus from the expansion of Western prestige and power, it also spearheaded the spread of Western knowledge, culture, and values."[243]

We have seen that early Presbyterian communities of the 19th century were predominantly European in their membership, governance, liturgy and architecture. When Māori, Asians and Pacific Islanders eventually joined, they had to fit into this Eurocentric model of church under the initial leadership of Europeans. However, this did not discount the influence of ethnic and cultural ties through those (non-European Christian converts) who evangelised their own people in more culturally relevant ways. In fact, their growing influence among their own people reflected an increasing desire for ethnic components to organise themselves in ways that encouraged their religio-ethnic identity.

A Eurocentric dynamic has enabled the European component to continue to be prominent in the PCANZ since its origins as a transplanted religious community from overseas. The Presbyterianism it held onto reinforced European values. But how could a Eurocentric model of church at the same time encourage ethnic homogeneity within the Māori, Asian and Pacific Islander components? One answer could lie in similar structures and processes of the PCANZ that governed them. There was a kind of cultural uniformity by virtue of their adoption of certain aspects such as moderator, clerk, and meeting procedures at local, regional and national levels. Māori, Asian and Pacific Islander components adopted elements of European Presbyterianism as part of establishing their religio-cultural identity. In this way of thinking, cultural agency occurs from the outside, effecting changes upon the receiving community. But this suggests that the receiving community is simply passive.

Arbuckle argues that the gospel needs to be "earthed" or inculturated by a community. Inculturation is "the dynamic relation between the Christian message and culture of peoples; an insertion of the Christian life into culture; an ongoing process of reciprocal and critical interaction and assimilation between them."[244] This process occurs within the local context of a people. The context, as Daniel Hardy sees it, is one in which there is a "braiding" or "interweaving" of the understanding of the gospel with the cultural life of the people.[245]

In this framework, contextualisation of the gospel is important for its genuine expression within the customs (including language) of a particular community. According to Lesslie Newbigin, it is through the cultural context of the Christian community that the gospel can transform the community's practices into ones that are faithful to the story of Christ in Scripture. "True contextualization happens when there is a community which lives faithfully by the gospel and in that same costly identification with people in their real situations as we see in the earthly ministry of Jesus."[246] Particular people groups are able to look critically at the form of Christianity they have received and begin to make distinctions between what is proper to the gospel according to the Scriptures and what is simply part of the traditional culture of those presenting it.[247]

What evolves, then, from within the new community is a Christian expression that is ethnically and culturally appropriate to the new context. This is, as Anne Keary notes, "establishing a connection with the colonizers on indigenous terms."[248] An interpretive process, or a "cultural hermeneutic" as Graham Ward puts it, also helps to transform a culture.[249] This occurs not only through the language and customs of that cultural context; it also includes the very people of that context. Presbyterianism was already culturally packaged when communicated into new cultural contexts of New Zealand, but those new contexts have reconfigured such cultural packaging of Presbyterianism so that it is recognised in ethnic-specific communities.

Whether the four components have developed through processes of enculturation, acculturation, adaptation, indigenisation, inculturation or contextualisation, the result is one in which they have eventually expressed a particular identity of themselves. For Māori and Asian components, although European Christians played a critical role in evangelism and establishment of early congregations, Māori and Asians, respectively, have since become the primary agents of development for their people. Similarly, the planting and spread of pan-Pacific congregations, and more recently island-specific congregations throughout New Zealand, came about largely, although not exclusively, through the efforts of Pacific Islanders themselves. The growing desire to live out their religiosity in culturally relevant ways, and the move toward greater autonomy (in terms of national bodies) seems to portray them as agents of cultural change. They have used their ethnic, cultural, ecclesial, and even familial connections to consolidate their church identity. Therefore, although the ethnic components operate as "Presbyterian," they portray themselves more markedly as European, Māori, Asian, and Pacific Islander Presbyterians.

The understanding of Presbyterianism as a European Christian denomination in New Zealand is clearly changing. The presence, growth and involvement of non-European groups in the PCANZ are signs of ongoing change. These are developments that shape how the PCANZ, as a national Church, can view itself in new ways. Although mainly referring to Christian missions, Andrew Walls' comment about the changing of Christian worldviews is helpful for our discussion: "The working out of Christian faith within accepted views of the world is so that those worldviews – as with the conversion of believers – are transformed, yet recognizable."[250] It seems that the worldview of the ethnic components of the PCANZ includes the high value of their ethnic/cultural identity that makes them "recognizable" – that is, distinct from others. Their identity is most apparent when they organise their religious life in ethnic-specific ways.

No matter how the ethnic components try to be faithful to the gospel message by critiquing and developing themselves, their practices inevitably demonstrate their own cultural perspectives. Even when change was initiated from the outside (in terms of European Christian influence) and accepted by Māori, Asians and Pacific Islanders, the consequence was not diverse congregations. Rather, they appropriated Presbyterianism in ways designed to clearly distinguish themselves from each other. These ways included the desire for worship services in the vernacular and for leadership of worshipping communities to reflect a distinctive cultural characteristic.

The result was the development of ethnic-specific Presbyterian communities. Whether they adapted European Christian ideas and practices or developed their own contextualised expression of the gospel, people from these communities were primarily the agents of their own development into homogeneous groups. The strong sense of belonging to one's own people, as well as a growing sense of ownership for one's religious community, affirms group identity and homogeneity. The desire to establish their own religio-cultural identity alongside those of others in the PCANZ was indicative of the importance of ethnic distinctions and cultural relevance. The practices of each component that encourage their homogeneity and relative autonomy as national bodies convey the perceived primacy of the ethnic component to which their members belong. This is in essence ethnocentrism.

All of this reflects an ethnocentrism that has encouraged a homogeneous legacy for the ethnic components of the PCANZ. The preference for one's own religio-ethnic identity creates a kind of separateness between the ethnic components. Ethnically homogeneous congregations within these components are, as Eric Law sees them, "ethnocentric towers." He makes an analogy with the story of the tower of Babel (Genesis 11: 1-9):

> In our separateness, we build our towers with our unspoken assumptions, values, and beliefs. As the towers get taller and taller, we create more distance and separation from others who are different. Up in our own tower, we create our own rituals that give us the illusion of certainty. Up in the imaginary security of our tower, we may conclude that our culture is God's culture."[251]

From this view, we can see that any development within an ethnic-specific congregation is one that promotes the cultural interests of its people. When ethno-cultural preferences are paramount for a congregation this discourages integration with others who are different and, instead, creates separation or distance from them. Even if a homogeneous religious community incorporates something from the outside into its life, it can transform it to affirm further the ethno-cultural aspirations of the community. When Christians remain within such a church culture (continuing to build up their tower) and have their religious life totally shaped by such a context, they become oblivious to the reality of a bigger context in which they are one amongst others. Such communities, as Law contends, "lose touch of what was going on in their changing communities on the ground."[252] It may be valid for the ethnic components of the PCANZ to organise themselves in ways that make the gospel and Christian traditions culturally appropriate and relevant for them, but if those ways encourage a kind of religio-ethnic superiority that segregates ethnic groups from each other or prevents constructive cross-cultural interaction, then how faithful is that to an ecclesiology of unity in diversity?

The initial Eurocentric thrust of Presbyterianism has gradually given way to an ethnocentric drive within the ethnic components. Although Europeans, Māori, Asians and Pacific Islanders in the PCANZ may function in the same way with regard to following regulations in the BOO, they clearly do so in ways that affirm their respective religio-ethnic identities.

Conclusion

In many ways the ecclesial development of the PCANZ reflects practices of ethnic and cultural parallels between peoples, particularly between clergy and congregations. Perhaps this is a consequence of mission practices that have attempted to be culturally grounded in texts like 1 Corinthians 9:19-23, where the Apostle Paul sums up by saying, "I have become all things to all people, that I might, by all means, save some" (v. 22). But if such practices are encased in a principle following McGavran that encourages homogeneous Christian communities, they also have the capacity to create a form of ecclesial separation which is contrary to a Christological and Trinitarian ecclesiology.

At the outset, Presbyterianism from Europe was transplanted to New Zealand primarily for early European settlers. Similarly, despite European initiatives with Māori, Asians, and Pacific Islanders, much of the growth of these components can be attributed to people from within these components. Using ethnic and cultural similarities as a basis for the establishment and development of the Christian church, they also encouraged ethnocentric tendencies in the life of the church. Again, there is a tension between church practices that affirm the effectiveness of ethnic and cultural parallels for the furtherance of the gospel and a theology that encourages diversity in the church.

More recently, as Stuart Vogel has rightly pointed out, the issue of immigration has had ramifications not only for the population of New Zealand, but also for its religious communities. With regard to

Asians and the PCANZ, Vogel asserts that "immigration patterns have already changed New Zealand and the local, regional, and national Presbyterian Church community in Aotearoa forever. We can and will never be the same again."[253]

That may be so in terms of the diversity of the PCANZ overall, but as the history of Asians in the PCANZ has shown us, it does not necessarily translate into diversity at the local congregation level. Even the bicultural relationship between European and Māori components is unclear. By and large it could be said that the two groups have inhabited largely separate worlds where there has not been a significant amount of shared involvement. As a result, Kevin Ward suggests, "it is questionable to what extent we have become a bicultural church, beyond the changing of our name to the Presbyterian Church of *Aotearoa* New Zealand."[254] Both of these points indicate that although the PCANZ is an ethnically and culturally diverse church, it does not always operate in ways that encourage diversity amongst its members, particularly within its congregations.

What I have presented does not amount to discrimination in the history of the PCANZ. However, we have seen that there have been entrenched prejudices in the development of the ethnic components – people in the PCANZ seem generally to prefer being with their own kind at the local level. Certain individuals stand out as examples of effective cross-cultural exchanges that support diversity between the ethnic components, but in the main, members of all components have preferred their religious activity to be amongst those who are like themselves. This may explain why ethnic relations among such groups in the national structure of the PCANZ today operate more in representative and consultative capacities than in relationships that encourage greater mixing between and within congregations of these components.

It remains to be demonstrated what the situation is today. There is no reason to think these historical patterns have changed. To be sure, we need to take a closer look at congregations today to measure the degree to which that is the case.

4 – Ethnic Relations in Congregations

What are PCANZ congregations really like? We saw earlier that, theologically, the local congregation reflects the unity in diversity of the church universal. We also observed how ethnocentric tendencies have shaped the ethnic components of the PCANZ. Despite this, there are intentions and attempts to reflect unity in diversity within the higher levels of PCANZ structures. But how is this reflected at the local level? What is the reality of ethnic relations within PCANZ congregations? I would like to paint a picture of this reality through details obtained from congregations from various presbyteries, as well as from questionnaires and interviews of parishioners and clergy.[255] They will assist us to identify the character of such congregations as well as how people order their religious activity in such contexts. This will provide some insight into the extent that ethnocentric tendencies impact our faith communities.

Homogeneous or Diverse?

Determining the ethnic homogeneity or diversity of a congregation is not easy. To assist us, we can revisit the 80/20 formula used by Emerson and Kim in their own research of congregations in the American context. To recap, a multiracial or diverse congregation is one in which no one racial group comprises 80% or more of the congregation.[256] Emerson used 20% as the "cut-off" because it constituted what he considered "the point of critical mass."[257] He states: "When a congregation has more than 20% of its membership from a minority group, then control and participation can begin to be shared among different ethnic groups."[258] Therefore, if one ethnic group makes up over 80% of a congregation, then that congregation could be defined as being ethnic-specific or homogeneous. If the balance is 80% or less, then that congregation could be considered ethnically diverse. This ratio, in my mind, is very generous in terms of categorising an ethnically diverse congregation, but for the sake of consistency with research done overseas it can be applied to congregations in our sample. We do not have to take this formula as being absolute for determining a congregation type, as if ethnic homogeneity and diversity are seen as a continuum, but merely as a tool to help provide a focus on the way we might generally identify them.

I examined details from 87 congregations comprising 14,537 people. The overwhelming majority were European (71%), followed by Pacific Islanders (18%), Asians (9%) and Māori (2%). Applying the above formula to these figures suggests that, because no one ethnic group has reached over 80% of the total number, the picture of the total people involved with such congregations is potentially colourful in terms of ethnic diversity.

However, applying the formula to the individual congregations to which these people belonged showed that the colours we noticed were not as rich as they first appeared. Of the congregation sample, 76 (83%) ended up being categorised as ethnically homogeneous. These congregations tended to be distinctively recognisable whereby they were either predominantly or exclusively European, Māori, Asian or Pacific Islander respectively. Only 15 (17%) were identified as being ethnically diverse. The figures clearly demonstrate that PCANZ congregations are inclined to be ethnically homogeneous rather than diverse. Although an earlier exploration of the New Zealand religious context only hinted at the possibility of diverse congregations in mainline Christian denominations, these results have confirmed the prevalence of ethnically homogeneous congregations and the scarcity of diverse ones in the PCANZ.

What we see here is an increasing clarity of what PCANZ congregations look like at present. Not only are the majority homogeneous, but they also portray a distinctive ethnic feature. People within these congregations do not gather together simply as Christians; rather, they apparently fellowship together as ethnically distinct Christian groups. They may have become part of these congregations for various reasons, but it seems the expression of their religious identity is also exercised through the affirmation of their ethnic and cultural identity.

Although church growth exponents like Donald McGavran and C. Peter Wagner have been criticised for their advocacy of homogeneous congregations, the reality of most congregations, both in the United States and in New Zealand through the PCANZ, is that they are clearly just that. Whether such congregations are more effective in terms of church growth is not the point here; instead, it is the fact that Christians appear to prefer demonstrating their religiosity in ethnic-specific ways. Ethnically diverse congregations, on the one hand, may be richer in terms of colour, ethnicity, culture, and ecclesiological expression; but on the other, they do not seem as popular, and are, therefore, significantly fewer in number and not so easily identified compared to homogeneous ones.

Moreover, I found (as Kevin Dougherty identified in the American context), that PCANZ congregations were more ethnically homogeneous than their general area populations. Although Europeans, Māori, Asians, and Pacific Islanders were represented in the populations of the areas in which they were located, their respective representations in PCANZ congregations were much higher. For example, although Europeans were predominant in the Wellington (67.7%), Christchurch (75.4%), and Dunedin (81.4%) regions, their numbers were more condensed in the congregations of the corresponding presbytery (Wellington 78.3%), (Christchurch 83.2 %), (Dunedin 88.3%).[259] The same was true for Māori who belonged to congregations within the areas covered by Te Aka Puaho, Asians in Wellington and Christchurch, and Pacific Islanders in Auckland and Wellington. Therefore, despite living in communities with others who may be ethnically different from themselves, Presbyterians seem to prefer exercising their religiosity with those who are similar to them. Perhaps the voluntary nature of the church accentuates this.

In terms of ethnically diverse congregations, it was no surprise that since the Auckland population had greater diversity, its presbytery (now known as the Northern Presbytery which includes the greater Auckland region) also had the highest number of diverse congregations (ten out of fifteen) compared to the other presbyteries. Despite this, there was still a slightly higher representation of homogeneous congregations in the Auckland presbytery indicating that, while some of the ethnic groups were found in diverse congregations, a much higher number were involved with congregations consisting mainly of their own ethnic group. This was especially so for Europeans, Māori and Pacific Islanders. A few diverse congregations were found in the other presbyteries, but the clear majority of congregations in them were ethnically homogeneous.

This shows that, despite the presence of diverse ethnic groups within the various regions, such ethnic identities tended to be represented more within the religious communities to which people belong. The prevalence of homogeneous congregations within relatively diverse areas suggests that people perhaps choose to commute across geographic boundaries to attend congregations that specifically affirm their religious and ethnic identity. Although this observation does not confirm this, the inference is there. Europeans, Māori, Asians, and Pacific Islanders within the PCANZ are inclined to align themselves with congregations in which their ethnic group is predominant or at least represented. Therefore, particular people groups tend to be more concentrated in their church congregations than they are in the general area where they live.

A closer look at these congregations revealed the extent of this homogeneity. Fifty-six congregations categorised as "European" consisted almost exclusively of Europeans. The total number of people within these congregations was 10,009. Of this number 9,440 (or 95%) were European. Of these 56 congregations, ten were exclusively European in membership, 30 had Europeans consisting between 90 to 99% of the congregation, while 16 had European membership of between 80 and 89%. Therefore, although a congregation could be categorised as "European" because more than 80% of its membership identified themselves as being of European descent, the clear majority of such congregations were almost completely European in representation.

Europeans are clearly the majority within PCANZ congregations. They tend to mirror their predominance not only in the wider geographical area in which they are located, but in the country as a whole of which they are the predominant culture within New Zealand society. Since the arrival, establishment, and development of Presbyterianism in New Zealand by early European settlers, they have continued to demonstrate their numerical strength in Presbyterian congregations. No doubt political and economic colonial powers have contributed to the religious strength of Presbyterian communities. But the fact that Europeans were instrumental in the founding and spread of these communities meant that they had the power to influence their growth. It could be that the homogeneity of European congregations today is just a reflection of their dominant numbers.

However, this homogeneity of European congregations might also be a consequence of an ethnocentric "hangover" from the past. We saw previously that Presbyterian congregations were intentionally set up in areas of the country settled by Europeans. Some settlements were established as Presbyterian communities. Even though the population of New Zealand has diversified considerably since the mid-1900s, PCANZ congregations have remained largely homogeneous. For European congregations in particular, they appear to have had a long history of maintaining the status quo. Therefore, just as there were ethnocentric tendencies that shaped European Presbyterian congregations in the past, it appears that those same tendencies may still be pervasive in European congregations today.

Non-Europeans, however, are present in European congregations. Despite the high representation of Europeans in their congregations and their prevalence in most regions of the PCANZ, other ethnicities in very small numbers have joined them. Forty six of the 56 European congregations had a few non-European people involved in them. This shows that notwithstanding the obvious homogeneity of European congregations, other ethnic minorities are still prepared to align themselves with such congregations. Whether this is due to family connections of spouses, English-language proficiency, worship style or proximity of the congregation is uncertain. Whatever their reasons for being part of such congregations, they are undoubtedly minorities.

Ten congregations in the sample I observed were categorised as being predominantly "Pacific Islander." Analogous to European congregations, Pacific Islanders were overwhelmingly represented

(94%) in these congregations. Six of the ten congregations consisted entirely of Pacific Islanders, while four included people of other ethnicities. The six exclusively Pacific Islander congregations consisted of those from a specific island group or nation. Two congregations consisted entirely of Samoans and Cook Islanders respectively, while one was represented wholly by Niueans. Only one congregation was pan-Pacific in that it had a significant representation of island groups or nationalities that included Samoans, Cook Islanders and Niueans. Despite the diverse character among island groups that a pan-Pacific congregation portrays, the clear conclusion is that Pacific peoples within the PCANZ render a partiality to church communities in which their Pacific roots are strongly represented.

Although Pacific peoples can fellowship together as "Pacific Islanders" in a generic sense, more of them appear to prefer a fellowship that is island-specific. The prevalence of island-specific congregations as opposed to pan-Pacific congregations clearly reveals the ethnocentric preferences of some Pacific peoples. While pan-Pacific congregations demonstrate a model of cross-cultural tolerance and sharing, the island-specific congregations are inclined to uphold greater identity distinctions and autonomy. Though this may prevent tensions with or interference from other island groups, these congregations also seem to reflect more of the dynamic of their home-island churches.

Considering their historical connections with the PCANZ, it is perhaps understandable why Pacific Islander congregations are just as homogeneous as European ones. Earlier we identified that Pacific Islander congregations and ministers first appeared on the scene in the PCANZ through their merger or incorporation from the CUNZ. They were not established by the PCANZ by means of mission, as with Māori or Asians. People from these Pacific Islander congregations were also "churched" from their respective island homelands. When coming into the PCANZ, they did so with a strong Pacific-church identity and background. Their relationship with the PCANZ began with clearly defined boundaries that set them apart from other ethnic components.

Similar to European congregations, the high degree of homogeneity within Pacific Islander congregations is still not an insurmountable barrier for non-Pacific folk. In four of these congregations, Europeans and Asians comprised five and one percent respectively. Three congregations included Europeans and Asians, while one reported having only Europeans as part of the congregation with Pacific Islanders. No Māori were represented in predominantly Pacific Islander congregations. Europeans, then, are more likely than Asians or Māori to participate in predominantly Pacific Islander congregations. Although my findings show non-Pacific folk involved with Pacific Islander congregations, it is only speculation as to whether the small numbers reflect inclusion of a spouse or if they represent a remnant of an ethnic group that was once predominant in a congregation's past.

Congregations categorised as "Māori" and "Asian" were also highly ethnic-specific in representation. The former consisted of 96% Māori with some European members included. The latter were entirely Asian in composition and of either Chinese or Korean membership respectively. Although Māori and Asians were identified in other congregation types, they were more concentrated in congregations categorised as "Māori" or "Asian."

A feature that Māori share with their ethnic counterparts is the effect of their historical development in the PCANZ. While they are represented by small numbers in other congregations, most Māori are inclined to reserve their religious activity to their own people. Not only do Māori congregations remain under the oversight of Te Aka Puaho as the Māori body or court of the PCANZ, they are also largely (though not totally) confined within a geographical or tribal region (Tuhoe), where they have very strong historical ties to the PCANZ and Māoridom. It is thus not surprising that these congregations are mainly ethnic-specific with respect to Māori.

Similarly, when Asian congregations, like some Pacific Islander ones, become extensions of churches from the homeland, they too have a propensity to be very ethnic-specific. The Korean congregations are such congregations and, even though incorporated into the PCANZ, they maintain strong and close links with other

Korean congregations in New Zealand and their Presbyterian Church denomination in Korea. Therefore, they tend to perpetuate a homogeneous dynamic. If this style of ministry and congregation life is what they are used to from the homogeneous church context of the homeland, then it stands to reason that such congregations are likely to continue practices that encourage an ethnic-specific development here in New Zealand. This demonstrates the tremendous effect that ethnic and cultural preferences can have upon religious communities.

Ethnic Group Predominance

The predominance of some ethnic groups were also seen in ethnically diverse congregations. Of the 1,555 people involved with such congregations, Europeans were the largest group, representing just over half (56%) of the membership in them, followed by Pacific Islanders (30%), Asians (11%) and Māori (3%). The majority of congregations had a mix of three or more ethnic groups involved. Europeans were represented in all 15 ethnically diverse congregations and were recorded as the largest ethnic group within ten of them, and equal largest with Pacific Islanders in one. To a slightly lesser degree, Pacific Islanders were represented in 13 of them and being the largest group in only two congregations while equal largest with Europeans in one. Asians followed by being represented in 11 congregations and having the largest number in just one of them. Māori were represented in six ethnically diverse congregations and also comprised the largest group in one of them. We can see that while diverse congregations have a wide mix of ethnicities involved, one group is usually larger than others. Again, this was particularly the case regarding Europeans. They appear to be a consistent factor within these types of congregations. But why is this?

Studying racially diverse religious organisations in the United States, Korie Edwards found that because race is central to how American society is organised, diverse churches needed to placate white members and affirm their religio-cultural preferences and interests in order to sustain their diversity.[260] Since whites are "culturally and structurally privileged and this privilege is normalized," Edwards argues that they are needed in diverse congregations to help them be successful.[261] Europeans in New Zealand society have been the dominant culture politically and economically since their arrival nearly 200 years ago. Their strength and influence within the PCANZ have clearly shaped Presbyterianism up to the present time. Although in-depth studies have not been done regarding ethnically diverse congregations in New Zealand, the presence of Europeans in all these diverse congregations may support Edwards' findings.

Previously we noted how research into religious communities within the United States found that ethnically diverse churches were rare. They were rare in terms of their diversity and lack of prevalence compared to homogeneous churches nationwide. This appears to be the case for PCANZ congregations as well. Similar to the other congregation types, historical developments have had a bearing on diverse congregations. The journey of Presbyterianism in New Zealand among its four main ethnic components has obviously been one influenced by ethnocentric tendencies that encouraged homogeneity rather than diversity within congregations. Despite attempts to integrate European congregations with Māori or Pacific Islanders, these efforts usually resulted in the groups reverting to a ministry that affirmed ethnic distinctions and separation.

In speaking with parishioners, it was very clear how ethnic and cultural connections between Christians shape the character of the congregations to which they belong. Adam has was involved with both ethnically diverse and pan-Pacific congregations. He is of European and Pacific Islander heritage, has a European spouse, and is very much at ease mixing with people of various ethnic and cultural backgrounds. When asked whether the ethnicity and culture of other fellow Christians influenced his sense of belonging in his congregation, he said:

> Absolutely; I totally believe that. It's a little more than even in my own theology. You know, we talk often about race as being a factor where people want a nice world where we can get together and worship together as one, but the truth, for me, is that you do gravitate towards where you feel most comfortable; where you contribute and feel part of a group. It tends, to me, to be closer to home and easier in a sense to have commonalities and connectedness rather than differences. It's like that with ethnicity or like-minded people.

Adam's comment suggests that the kind of congregation people involve themselves with may be the consequence of their partiality to what is "most comfortable" ethnically and culturally for them rather than their theological understanding of the church. Having a sense of comfort can mean involvement in either a homogeneous community or a diverse one. But if "commonalities and connectedness rather than differences" are some of the key aspects for belonging in a community, such aspects are likely to be lived out within ethnically homogeneous communities instead of diverse ones.

Even within diverse congregations, there can be a tendency to keep one's associations with one's own people. Darren is European and his situation seems to reflect this dynamic.

Darren:

> At this church we have Taiwanese and Samoan … but there are a number of Chinese people who have chosen to join the Pakeha [European] congregation; not many, probably two or three families. So really, I don't have a lot of social contact with people who are of a different ethnicity to me.

Graham is a Samoan who had long associations with an exclusively Samoan congregation. Since his tertiary education, employment, and social activities exposed him to more ethnic and cultural diversity, he wanted to experience this in his church life. But when choosing a new congregation to worship, the level of diversity went only as far as a pan-Pacific congregation.

Graham:

> When we made that decision we believed that we could still associate with some Samoan people, but mainly there were Pacific Islands people. Not only introducing myself into that organisation or group of people, there were Samoans who could understand me and who could respect me. At the same time I thought that after being there for a while I could learn more about ways of worship with other Pacific people.

On the other hand, Dianna, a Korean, appreciated the transition from an all-Korean church into one where she was an ethnic minority.

Dianna:

> I enjoyed the differences and I still enjoy worshipping in English because I got used to it. It is definitely different to worship in English; you cannot get that same feeling when worshipping in Korean. I enjoyed the people of this land and they are again a bit different. There are a lot of things I can learn from and also participate in and enjoy. For me, it was a good experience in both churches and I'm still doing it now.

These comments demonstrate varying approaches people can take toward ethnic relations and the kind of congregation in which they participate. They particularly say something about the kinds of people they engage with. The vast majority of parishioners interviewed shared that they appreciated the importance of good communication and cultural relevancy. Regardless of whether or not a parishioner was ethnically matched with a specific group, positive and relevant connections with that group were very influential for associations. However, since most parishioners related mainly with their own ethnic group, the high regard for good social connections could also be reflective of ethnic connections. In other words, parishioners may experience better communication and social connections and feel more comfortable within such groups because of ethnic and cultural parallels.

It was no surprise then that these strong socio-cultural connections were manifested in ethnic-specific ways within subgroups of congregations. Details from congregations also highlighted that ethnic representation in the leadership group (Session or Parish Council) of most congregations generally reflected that of their membership.[262] This meant that some were diverse while most were ethnically homogeneous. The consequence was that the largest ethnic group in a congregation was inclined to have greater representation in the leadership group, and therefore made it seem more ethnic-specific in nature. Similarly, within ethnically diverse congregations the leadership tended to be relatively less diverse than that of congregation membership.[263] Of the four ethnic components examined, Europeans, more than any other group, were inclined to be involved with the leadership of their respective congregations, regardless of whether or not their membership number was larger or smaller than other ethnic groups. In some ways, this may, again, reflect Edwards' view about the dominant and advantaged status and culture of Europeans in New Zealand society being worked out within religious communities, particularly ethnically diverse ones.

This dynamic can be reflected in any sub-group of a congregation. But when sub-groups are inclined to becoming ethnically exclusive they can not only marginalise minorities, they can also make them seem invisible. Practices like this, even if unintentional, can say something about the ethnic and power dimensions within the life of the congregation. They can show how the culture of a congregation can be influenced by the culture of the majority group. This was demonstrated in Harry's congregation with regard to the management committee. It consisted entirely of Europeans despite the congregation having a significant number of Māori and Asians.

Harry:

> I don't know why that is because everybody seems to fit in. The management committee, when I originally went onto it, was looking for business people to manage the church or be responsible or have a rough idea of involvement with money; what to do when something was broken and that. [It was] trying to get the right people in the right place. I mean, you know, there are Māori and Asians who are also in business, but I don't know why they are not, you know, on it.

Today the presence of diverse congregations indicates some small progress in ethnic relations between Europeans, Māori, Asians, and Pacific Islanders of the PCANZ. They demonstrate that despite the long history of homogeneity in congregations, ethnic diversity is possible. Perhaps they also reflect the increasing ethnic and cultural diversity that is developing in New Zealand society. Having ten diverse congregations located in the Auckland area may mirror the diversity of the population there, but it does not explain why there are not more of them. Despite this, the presence of diverse congregations is a hopeful sign of change that there are some churches trying to live out the PCANZ's ecclesiology of unity in diversity at the local level.

Worship Services

In my ministry experiences at Otara PIC and First Church of Otago, there were numerous worship services every Sunday. In both contexts, people from different ethnic groups would fellowship together in a combined worship service conducted mainly in English (though incorporating other languages), but most usually participated in a service conducted in their own vernacular and attended mainly by those with the corresponding ethnicity. Worship services, then, can be indicators of the ethnic dynamics in these congregations. What might worship services in other congregations reveal about their ethnic dynamics?

Most congregations I examined had one worship service only, but a few had multiple services ranging from two to as many as five. The clear majority (88%) of congregations indicated having worship services conducted in English, but these were confined to those categorised as European, Pacific Islander and diverse. It must be noted here that some Māori and Pacific Islander congregations indicated some use of English in their respective worship services, but in the main their vernacular was preferred.

It was not surprising that all European congregations had English-language worship services. Only one congregation indicated having another worship service conducted in a Pacific language. Ethnic representation of those who attended worship services conducted in English reflected that of a congregation's membership, which meant that attendees were mainly European. This was to be expected since they were the predominant group in most of these congregations. Non-Europeans also attended these worship services conducted in English, but this was probably due more to the fact that such services were the only ones available in their respective congregations rather than due to their proficiency with English. In the sole European congregation that had one other service conducted in a Pacific language, those members whose ethnicity corresponded with that language were the only ones who attended that service. While some of these Pacific Islanders also attended the English-language service, nearly all of them attended the service conducted in their language. Conversely, no Europeans attended the Pacific-language service in this congregation. This indicates that, given a choice of worship services in a particular language, people are inclined to attend services in which their ethnic and cultural identity is affirmed.

Parallels were also noted within some Pacific Islander congregations. Some indicated having a worship service in English as well as others in particular island-languages. But what is noteworthy is that while some Pacific Islanders attended the English-language service in their congregation, a much higher proportion were recorded in attendance at the respective island-language services. Again, the homogeneous dynamic of such services may signal issues of language proficiency, but they might also affirm the ethnic and cultural identity of those who attend the service. The two are in many ways inseparable.

Diverse congregations mainly had worship services conducted in English while some also held worship services in other languages. Ethnic representation at the English-language worship services showed relative consistency with congregation membership. More striking is the fact that European members were better represented at English-language services than their Māori, Asian and Pacific Islander counterparts. As well as their relatively high number within nearly two-thirds of diverse congregations, their predominance in English-language services may also be due to the fact that those congregations had only one such service. In this sense the English language of Europeans as the majority group became the language for the rest in their worship services.

This is an aspect that Kathleen Garces-Foley observed about evangelical multiethnic churches in the United States. She explains that although creating a formidable language barrier for most new immigrants, English as a common language has "enabled these churches to avoid the division into linguistic groups that greatly deters cross-cultural interactions."[264] In a similar vein, Edwards' identification of the influence of whites in racially diverse congregations adds that the "culture and structures" of diverse churches (blacks and whites) affecting "nearly every measure of worship practices and congregational activities" were more consistent with white churches rather than black churches.[265] These points seem to be paralleled in the diverse congregations of the PCANZ.

Four diverse congregations also had worship services conducted in other languages. Three respectively incorporated particular Pacific-language services, while one included a service conducted in an Asian language. Regardless of the diversity of these congregations, people attending such services were only those whose ethnicity corresponded with the particular language in which the service was conducted. Attendance at such services was very ethnic-specific, which highlights again how worship services can be indicators of ethnic relations.

Some parishioners have clear views about how cultural identity is reflected in the worship setting. Carol is part of a pan-Pacific congregation and attends a combined service led in English where she has the opportunity to fellowship with other Pacific peoples. But she tends to appreciate a Cook Islanders' service that is more meaningful and relevant for her.

Carol:

> I said before I can relate better to other Cook Islanders. The other thing is about wanting to express yourself in worship with other Cook Islanders because we have things in common that I don't have with, say, Samoans or Niueans. It's where I come from; you know, it has to do with our traditions and language. I think there is a need too to support my Cook Islanders' community. I mean, we are a small group and so we should be supporting one another, you know.

Harry belongs to a predominantly European congregation with non-European minorities represented. Although everyone attended the only worship service conducted in English, he comments on the ethnic divisions still noticeable through how they seated themselves: "So, I have to admit, we sit on this side of the church and they on that side and you don't really hear what people say." Harry's comment suggests that despite the mix of people represented in a worship context, they may still exercise their preferred way of fellowship in more ethnically distinctive patterns.

By and large, it appears that ethnic relations in churches are also exemplified through the kinds of worship services that people attend. The language in which a worship service is conducted may also have some influence upon the kinds of people who choose to attend them. If conducted in the language of the majority group of a congregation, then, as I have shown, those who attend are inclined to have an ethnicity that corresponds to that language. Those whose ethnicity does not correspond may attend because they have some command of the language in which the worship service is conducted or because it is the only service available to them. Therefore, while some parishioners try to be involved in a worship setting where they perhaps do not fit ethnically and culturally, the vast majority prefer similarity and familiarity.

Clergy and Congregations

One of the interesting features of the pan-Pacific congregation in which I grew up and eventually served as a minister was the ethnic and cultural relationship between the ministers and the island groups of the congregation. Each of us three ministers was ethnically matched with one of the island groups. We shared responsibilities together in combined events of the three island groups, but our main area of ministry was among the group with whom we shared the same ethnicity. The rationale was that church ministry would be better served by the ethnic and cultural compatibility between minister and congregation group. I wondered if other churches experienced a similar dynamic of ethnic matching between minister and congregation.

Part of the details obtained from congregations concerned the ethnicity of clergy. The majority of congregations had a sole minister serving within them while some had two and fewer still had three or more ministers. Only four congregations did not have a minister. In terms of ethnic representation, European ministers comprised almost three-quarters of the total number (103) of ministers, followed to a much lesser extent by Pacific Islanders, Māori and Asians.[266]

What I discovered was that there was a clear correlation between the ethnicity of clergy and the predominant group of a congregation. Ninety one percent of European congregations had European ministers serving in them, while the rest either had a non-European minister or no minister at the time. What we see here is a very high ethnocentric dynamic at work in European church ministries that is evident in the relationship between minister and congregation.

Although similarities were seen in Māori and Asian congregations, it was also particularly noticeable within Pacific Islander ones. Pacific Islander congregations that were exclusively Samoan and Cook Islander also had Samoan and Cook Islander ministers respectively. A congregation consisting of a Samoan and Tongan group also had two ministers: a Samoan and a Tongan. Similarly, one congregation that had Samoans and Europeans (among other ethnic groups) also had two ministers: a Samoan and a European. One pan-Pacific congregation consisting of Samoans, Cook Islanders and Niueans (with the Samoan group being the largest of the three island groups) had a Samoan as their minister. Therefore, ethnic matching nonetheless appears to be prevalent.

There was more diversity in the ethnic representation of clergy serving in ethnically diverse congregations. But, as in pan-Pacific churches, the correlation between the ethnicity of minister and the largest group was also seen in diverse congregations. Of the congregations in which Europeans were the larger ethnic group among others, 70% had European ministers. Those in which Pacific Islanders were the larger ethnic group each had a Pacific Islander minister also. The same was also true for those in which Asians and Māori were the larger group among others. This relationship shows that despite the ethnic diversity of such congregations there is a propensity for clergy who serve in them to share the same ethnicity as that of the largest group in the congregation. It appears to affirm an ethnic and cultural dynamic for a majority ethnic group within a congregation.

The ethnic parallel between clergy and the predominant ethnic group of a congregation was also seen in the way they related. I found that most parishioners who engaged more often with their minister tended to be ethnically matched with them. This was not surprising given the ethnic homogeneity of congregations and the ethnic parallel with clergy. The converse was true for most ethnic minorities in such congregations. Even details from clergy regarding engagement with parishioners also affirmed this. Yet, there were some exceptions of clergy and parishioners who were not ethnically matched having high levels of interaction. These cases suggested that ethnic differences did not hinder such relations. Although this is encouraging, they were rarer.

The positive relations between parishioner and minister who are ethnically matched are reflected in Florence's experience. When asked how she found relating with her current minister, Florence replied: "Oh, wonderful. She's one of those people that just fitted in straight away. She was one of us." The last part of her comment can be interpreted in different ways, but having the minister being "one of us" can also include the ethnic parallel. This was clearly seen in Carol's pan-Pacific congregation where, despite having three ministers of different island ethnicities, she was more inclined to engage mostly with the one with whom she was ethnically matched.

Carol:

I think, to be honest, I have a particular leaning towards the Cook Islander minister. Yeah, I think I'm more inclined to talk more and interact more with our Cook Islander minister because ... it's only been our Cook Islander minister that's visited me or counselled me about anything; yeah, not the other two. Again, I think I would be more comfortable with our own minister anyway because, you know, we are the same ... It's not that I haven't appreciated the work of our other ministers, because I do. But I think it does matter ... people respond differently depending on that connection with the minister.

However, it has to be said that interaction between minister and parishioner is not purely based upon ethnicity. Much of it also has to do with the needs of people. Though true this may be, the pervasiveness of ethnocentric tendencies suggest that they are still significant lenses through which pastoral needs are seen or addressed. Yet this trend can be occasionally bucked. This was the case for Jay, a European minister, who served in a predominantly European congregation with a small number of Asian and Pacific Islander members.

Jay:

Visiting is perhaps the wrong word; pastoral contact probably covers it more. I have probably put more emphasis on the non-Europeans in some ways because there is actually quite a strong group of younger Koreans and one Fijian girl here. I try to spend more time with them, especially last year, to build them up, but that was not simply because of their different ethnicity; it was more because of the age they were. I have a particular ministry with tertiary students and that's what they were, and they were Asian.

The ethnocentric dynamic within congregations can also shape clergy. Exploring the extent of this in their church experiences prior to, during, and post-ministry training exposed some very revealing insights. Before training for church ministry, nearly all (97%) ministers, as parishioners then, indicated that they came from congregations that consisted predominantly or exclusively of people with the same ethnicity as them. Similar to what we saw above, most of them (88%) were also ethnically matched with the minister in their congregation. Consequently, they were inclined to associate mainly with others with whom they had ethnic and cultural parallels. These tendencies may also mirror the fact that the overwhelming majority of ministers (94%) indicated having a spouse with whom they were also ethnically matched. Accordingly, before entering ministry training, ministers (as parishioners) already had a predisposition to relate generally with people of their own kind.

This tendency was also manifested in their experiences during their training for church ministry. Clergy pointed out that, as ministry students, they were exposed to ethnic diversity in terms of other ministry students and staff within their own training institution as well as in other learning institutions. However, despite engaging with fellow students who were ethnically dissimilar, they were inclined to interact more with those with whom they shared the same ethnicity. This was perhaps inevitable for European students who were part of the predominant ethnic group.[267] While Māori, Asian and Pacific Islander students, as ethnic minorities during ministry training greatly valued their relations with European students, they also indicated a higher level of engagement with their own kind. Though generally appreciative of their fellow ministry students during their years of training for ministry, at a deeper and more personal level the way clergy organised themselves, whether intentionally or not, did raise awareness of ethnic similarity and difference between them. For example, Matthew is a New Zealand-born Samoan who had been part of a pan-Pacific congregation. He considered that he genuinely engaged well with all ministry students, but outside of classes (in his own time) he found himself involved more with other Samoan students.

Matthew:

I'll be honest, I think I spent more time with the Samoan students and then with other Pacific Islanders, and then with the Europeans. In saying that, I was quite close with the Māori students. Two of them were there and one of them went through assessment with me. We had a special bond, but it was mainly with the Samoan students.

For Xavier, being the only Māori student amongst other student ethnicities meant that his exposure to diversity was marked. In acknowledging this aspect, his minority status made this experience one of alienation as well.

Xavier:

One time we finished a lecture ... For that moment I felt really lonely. What happened was, we all came out and all these Pakehas turned to other Pakehas and started talking, and that was good. All the Samoans turned to each other and started talking in Samoan ... Niueans all turned to each other and started talking Niuean... I turned to speak Māori to someone and there was nobody else. That was the first time I felt lonely. Everyone was conversing in their own languages with their own people and I had no one to converse with in Māori... That forced me out to meet other Māori people in Dunedin. That has always stuck in my mind.

From these comments, we can see that the representation of different ethnicities provided opportunities for diverse relations during the ministry training of ministers. But we also heard that despite the positive view of diversity among ministry students, there was still a trend of gravitating towards those with whom they were ethnically similar.

This dynamic was also demonstrated in the kind of congregation they attended during their ministry training years. With the freedom of choice for a congregation to join, the clear majority of clergy, as ministry students, indicated joining a congregation in which their ethnic group was predominant.[268] Although some specified that they were ethnic minorities in their congregations, they also revealed that they were in fact ethnically matched with a minority group in the congregation. A clear majority of them also conveyed an ethnic parallel with the minister of the congregation. Therefore, regardless of being part of a minority or majority group, most ministry students tended to join congregations in which their ethnic group was represented. Despite some ministry students who experienced diverse ethnic relations in their congregations during their training for ministry, most were inclined to continue a degree of homogeneity in their religious relations. This suggests that whatever other reasons they may have had for joining such congregations, ethnic and cultural preferences appear to be quite influential upon their decision. Most clergy, as ministry students, experienced the tension between their theological training and the reality of their relations with others. Although they attempted to exercise diversity in their relationships with fellow students, they continued affirming a homogeneous dynamic in their church life.

Considering the ethnocentric tendencies in their church experiences prior to and during their ministry training, what kind of congregation would the ministry students envisage beginning their church ministry? Would their theological and practical training about church and ministry reflect a change to their perceptions and practices regarding the kinds of people their ministry would serve? By this I mean a change from homogeneous ethnic relations to diverse ones.

Clergy were reasonably clear on the kind of congregation in which they wanted to begin their church ministry. Those who had a preference of serving in a congregation with whom they were ethnically matched with the majority of parishioners was the popular choice for a slight majority (39%). Although fewer envisaged ministry in ethnically diverse congregations where their ethnic group was at least represented (15%), fewer still wanted to serve in congregations where they were clearly a minority (6%). This was particularly evident among European ministers of which none wanted the latter context. It seemed more preferable to serve in a congregation where clergy were either ethnically matched with the predominant group or with at least one of the ethnic groups within it. Hardly any of them wanted to be in a ministry situation where they were out of their comfort zone as an ethnic minority. Yet, a significant number (36%) indicated not having a preference about the ethnic composition of the congregation to which they would serve in ministry. European and Pacific Islander ministers were evenly split in this respect. This was surprising since many obviously had ethnic preferences about being part of a particular congregation prior to and during ministry training. However, the fact that these respondents expressed no preference may suggest that the ethnic element of a congregation was not a primary consideration compared to other factors, like a congregation's geographical location or suitable schooling for children and spouse employment.

The following responses perhaps reveal the convictions of clergy. For Basil, despite attending an ethnically diverse congregation during his ministry training, the ethnic representation of a congregation was not as significant for him as the theological stance and missional drive of the congregation.

Basil:

I suppose at that stage it was more a church of what you [might] call a theological mix that was given more consideration. Also, a progressive church or an innovative church; they would have been the prime considerations.

But for others like Venice and Victor, a Pacific Islander and Māori respectively, returning to church ministry among their own people was very much part of their consideration.

Venice:

Well, I was a big dreamer when I came out [from ministry training]. I had gone in thinking, I mean I got my calling when I was in the P.I.C. church and I would love to come back to P.I.C. churches. I know how difficult it is for women to get into a P.I.C. church, but I thought it would happen; it's just a matter of when. So I would have loved to come back to a P.I.C. church ... I wasn't really thinking about going into a Palagi (European) church at all.

Victor:

At the end of my preparation [for ministry], the parish that I wanted to go back to was a Māori parish. I felt that our people needed our own people to be part of them to help them come through, you know, their community and the physical and spiritual side... I was looking to the future of our people ... That's why I thought I would go back into a [Māori] Synod parish.

There may be various reasons for the kind of congregation or ministry in which clergy sought to serve, yet ethno-cultural commonalities were still clearly influential factors irrespective of location, theological views, or missional and worship styles of congregations. Given that ministers had a history of homogeneous experiences in their congregational life, it is not surprising that many envisaged continuing that dynamic in their parish ministry. For those with aspirations of a new experience within diverse congregations, or ones in which they were an ethnic minority, perhaps this was shaped by their theological education about church and ministry.

However, envisaging one's ministry is one thing; the reality of it is another. The outcomes for these clergy were very different from what they had earlier anticipated as ministry students. Of those who earlier expressed an overt desire to begin their ministry in a congregation predominantly of their same ethnicity, the number who ended up in this situation nearly doubled (70%). Surprisingly, although only a small number aspired to serve in a context that was largely ethnically dissimilar to them, more than twice as many experienced this reality (15%). Those who wanted to begin parish ministry in an ethnically diverse church remained almost the same (12%).

A closer look at this comparison revealed some interesting findings. The increase of the number of ministers who ended up in an ethnically matched situation with their respective congregation occurred only amongst European ministers. This increase came from half of the European ministers who earlier wanted to serve in an ethnically diverse congregation, but more so from those who previously indicated that they had no particular preference. It should not be seen as something unexpected since we saw earlier that no European minister wanted to serve in a congregation as an ethnic minority. The opposite may have been the case for the very few in the very early days of the establishment of Māori, Asian, and Pacific Islander congregations, but not in more recent times. Today it seems that the vast majority of European clergy prefer a ministry among their own kind. Pacific Islander ministers on the other hand were more inclined than others to serve in congregations that were either ethnically diverse or in which they were the ethnic minority.

Our plans do not always work out the way we want, but these results may also reveal unspoken or subconscious preferences, particularly amongst European clergy who, despite indicating no preference of a congregation type, all ended up in congregations which were predominantly European. This is not surprising since they had consistently demonstrated ethnocentric tendencies in their congregation experiences prior to and during their ministry training. To be fair, however, the reality could have been that these were the only kinds of congregations available and open to them.

There are obviously all sorts of things that can determine what kind of congregation a minister will serve in. The sense of call is also discerned by the receiving congregation. But the above observations seem to indicate that ethnic preferences are surely, though not an openly spoken, part of a minister's consideration for accepting or not accepting to serve in a particular kind of congregation. Comments by Basil and Sheri, who are both European and who started their ministries in predominantly European congregations, highlight this point.

Basil:

I mean there would have been no point [in] me considering going into a Pacific Islanders church because, if you like, at that stage there were more Pacific Islands ministers than there were churches. So for Pacific Islander ministers going through the training, the chances of them getting a Pacific Islands church would have been very, very slim. They would have been ... going more than likely into a European church. So that wasn't really a consideration for me.

Sheri:

It's interesting. I never really thought that much about ethnicity. I was thinking of size in terms of where I wanted to go, and location. I thought I would like to stay in the South Island and be in a medium size town; nothing too small, nothing too big. But I ended up in Auckland ... I don't know if I specifically thought about it, but mind you, I probably just assumed that I would be in a mainly predominantly European parish, yeah.

In Basil's case, his comment for discounting serving in a largely Pacific Islander congregation could be understood as illustrating the practicalities of a relevant ministry or the reality of the types of congregations there are in the PCANZ. But it might also be seen an indirect attempt to omit his preference for ministry among Europeans. In Sheri's case it could be a matter of "colour-blindness" by unconsciously continuing within a church context she had been used to.

The movement of ministers from one congregation ministry to the next also appeared to work along ethnic and cultural lines. European ministers particularly were more inclined to serve consecutively in parishes where their own ethnic group was predominant. The movement of Pacific Islander ministers in the sample was different. Two-thirds began their ministry in mainly European congregations while the other third served in Pacific Islander congregations. However, most serving in European congregations eventually moved onto predominantly Pacific Islander ones. Pacific Islander ministers, more than their other ethnic cohorts, leaned to serving parishes in which they were an ethnic minority. It could be that European ministers chose to serve in predominantly European congregations because there were simply more of them than non-European ones. It could also be that Pacific Islander ministers served in European parishes because there were not enough Pacific Islander parishes to go around, as Basil had earlier noted. If both cases are true, it suggests that ministers are perhaps limited in their choice for the kind of parish in which they may really wish to serve. However, if given options, their track record suggests they would nonetheless be inclined to choose a church ministry mainly among their own kind. This is highlighted more by the fact that not only did ministers tend to serve in congregations where their ethnic group was represented, but almost all these groups were also predominant.

Again, what we have just noted affirms the correlation between the ethnicity of a minister and that of the majority ethnic group of a congregation. In the few cases where they were not matched with such a congregation, these ministers at least shared the same ethnicity with one of the other minority groups in the congregation. Apart from the latter, the parish ministry of most clergy tended to be limited to those who were the same as them.

In sum, a minister may choose to serve in a particular congregation for all kinds of reasons, but connecting relevantly with its members regardless of their ethnicity is very crucial for effective ministry. When ministers are not able or unwilling to improve their cross-cultural relations, it becomes easier to confine their ministry amongst those with whom they are ethnically and culturally matched. Again, this echoes the research of Emerson that there is much more work and cost entailed in ministries within multi-ethnic congregations. This is clearly conveyed in Sam's experience of ministry in a pan-Pacific congregation.

Sam:

> Because I am Cook Islander there is some common understanding between myself and my people about what and how we do things. Our bond, so to speak, is already in place, whereas to connect myself to the Samoan world or the Niuean world is much harder. I have to push myself more to make those connections. Language is certainly one of those things to work at ... So there are bridges that have to be built so that a relation can be established between myself and the Samoan or Niuean portion of the church. I've also had to learn the different cultural protocols for different occasions and that's not easy either.

Drawing on the incarnational theology of Christ, Basil argues that a minister, regardless of ethnicity, must be adaptable in order to work within the cultural context of the congregation.

Basil:

> But actually what works is putting it into a theological paradigm, that is, if you want, "the Word became flesh and dwelt among us." The incarnation was God dwelling with his people. In other words taking on human form and taking on human flesh. So I would say that a minister, no matter where he is ministering, must be incarnational in the culture in which he finds himself. And if you are not incarnational within that particular culture, then you haven't got a ministry.

On one hand, ministers may feel more adequate in an ethnic-specific context that encourages the religious life of the people in culturally relevant ways, but consequently continues to affirm homogeneity. On the other hand, being part of an ethnically diverse congregation may be more faithful to our ecclesiology but can be very challenging and demanding in terms of connecting relevantly and effectively with those who are ethnically and culturally different from the minister. This tension in terms of theology and practice in church ministry is articulated in the responses of Venice and Peter, who are both Pacific Islanders. Venice saw the importance of cultural relevancy that also affirmed ethnic homogeneity; but for Peter, ethnic diversity in a congregation meant no room for separatism or ethnic distinctions between peoples.

Venice:

That's where my heart is, to go back to the P.I.C. church, and who else can minister to them better than people who can relate to them even more? I mean, it does factor in, in terms of relating to people and knowing their background, whereas having someone outside of your culture come in and try and relate the gospel in a way that's very foreign and unusual, and they themselves couldn't understand. That's the problem with colonialism, wasn't it?

Peter:

One of the problems is that when you start in that direction of separate language services you can become a family that sits in its own corner. Again, that's not my theology. I think you create family where everyone can work together without having to set time slots in the afternoon to do their own thing ... When we talk about multicultural we also have to talk about integration. We can't divide up the church. We can have multiculturalism but not separateness ... Sure, there will be the temptation, you know, "I want to talk in my language," but I think that if it's about God's work then it should be a work that allows people to be together without boundaries of language or culture or protocols.

Most European ministers interviewed were more conscious about this matter. While some clearly saw the benefits of a homogeneous relationship, many were not convinced that this relationship should define a congregation. Like Peter, their idea of church was one in which Christians should not be divided along ethnic or cultural lines; rather, they should be united by their identity in Christ.

Jay:

I always had an idea of building a multi-ethnic church. I'm not quite sure why, but that's what I thought church should be. I'm not a great fan of separation so I'm not even a great fan of having separate congregations or services, you know, in Cook Islands or Māori ... I can see why it happens and I guess there is some value in it, but I think we need to work harder at being Christian together.

Basil:

I could start an ethnic church tomorrow, but we've got a major problem. I'm very much into diversity in the body of Christ and very supportive of, if you like, the special needs of our various cultural groups. Yet to the greatest extent it's a form of apartheid in my view. It's doing us far more harm than good and it's actually separating us... While we have special groups for some Asian people or for some Indians ... our goal is to actually build relationships with each other. Our goal is to integrate rather than separate.

Ministers are very much aware of and embrace the theology of the unity in diversity of the church, particularly as a way of preventing or limiting separation amongst peoples in the congregation. The ecclesiology we have already explored is the ideal of the church that its members strive towards. But the critical point is how that ideal is lived out as faithfully as possible. Basil pointed out that the goal of integration was to build relationships amongst people in the congregation. But without the integration of people's cultural elements into the shared life and culture of the congregation, is this really integration? Surely the integration of new cultures will change the current culture. Or is it more about the assimilation of new cultures into the existing culture of the congregation, assimilation into a European culture that stands for Christian culture? What seems clear is the idea of unity in which people can belong together in a Christian congregation. What is debatable is the kind of unity that congregations want to live out. Is it a unity in diversity or homogeneity?

Does an incarnational theology mean that ministers should encourage congregational practises that affirm homogeneity because they are grounded in homogeneous contexts? Not necessarily. Just as Christ became flesh to exercise God's purpose of grace and reconciliation to all of humanity, so too is this the case for ministry. It is about the God of community who is embodied in Jesus in order to bring all people into community with one another and with God. In essence, an incarnational theology is transformative. Therefore, applying it to ministry does not mean a fixture of homogeneity within a community, but a transformation of that community into one that reflects the unity in diversity of God.

This is where the tension lies. It seems easier or more preferable for people of similar ethnicities to fellowship together than it is for those who are ethnically different. The former, therefore, might explain why homogeneous congregations are prevalent in the PCANZ and why ethnically diverse ones are scarce. In both cases there is Christian unity, but homogeneous congregations seem to portray a particular kind of unity. It is one that might bring a sense of meaning and comfort to a particular majority, but the homogeneous dynamic also means that it is largely an exclusive unity that is not consistent with the inclusive diversity that the PCANZ claims for itself. Ethnically homogeneous congregations have an incomplete unity that needs further transformation.

The tension is also a challenge to ministers about how their ministries can shape their congregations. If they believe in and confess the unity in diversity of the church, then surely they should be working towards reflecting that in the ministries of their congregations. Basil's earlier comment that ministers who do not work towards this goal do not have a ministry may be extreme, but he has a point. There must be some consistency in the way church practises reflect its ecclesiology.

Conclusion

I have attempted to identify what kind of image local congregations really reflect of the PCANZ. What I see is a mosaic. While a few ethnic representations in some congregations mirrored the theological unity in diversity that the PCANZ affirms of itself, the vast majority were in reality homogeneous. The colourful mosaic of diversity is in fact the collective presence of homogeneous congregations within it. Most congregations in themselves are not so colourful. Even within congregations that are pan-Pacific, particular island ethnicities can be prominent over others. Therefore, while the picture we see from a distance can seem ethnically kaleidoscopic, up close it is rather monochromatic.

Parishioners may believe in the Christian unity they have with one another, but that unity appears to be lived out in ethnic-specific ways within their congregations. It can become a congregational culture or practice that is assumed to be acceptable because it occurs within a Christian community context. To some extent it is, but it is not the totality of our theological understanding of the church. Yet the ethnocentric tendencies of parishioners seem to shape the homogeneity of their congregations. Even when they have the opportunity to build up diverse ethnic relations with minority groups in their congregation, these tendencies usually encourage them to revert to relations that are familiar and comfortable. Perhaps the challenges and costs of cross-cultural experiences or efforts to try to diversify their relationships in the congregation are too great an obstacle for them. Whatever their reasons, they seem sufficient to convince most parishioners that their homogeneous religious context is the place they belong.

Such a view of congregations clearly reflects the dynamic of ethnic parallels of relationships within congregations. Of particular significance to my exploration is the pattern of ethnic matching identified between clergy and the largest ethnic groups of congregations. Despite aspects such the sense of call and suitability or compatibility between minister and congregation, the findings about this relationship suggest that it is also, to a large degree, drawn along ethno-cultural lines. Such a relationship may also indicate a preference or bias for ethnic parallels, either from the perspective of the congregation or from the minister, or both. The prevalence of ethnic matching strongly implies that the ministry within it is perhaps more effective in terms of ethnic and cultural relevancy, or that it demonstrates a form of colour-blindness where such a relation of ethnic matching is taken as the norm in church ministry.

What is very interesting is that despite the theological conviction of ministers about the unity in diversity of the church, many were still inclined to serve in congregations that were largely homogeneous. The ministry situation of most ministers is one that apparently supports ethnic similarity. Thus, although many ministers may aspire to the unity in diversity of the church and ministry as an ideal, the reality for most of them is the comfort and familiarity of homogeneous congregations. This is a pressing issue not just for ministers but for the PCANZ as a whole.

Overall, the picture that is becoming increasingly apparent about the PCANZ through its congregations is one that differs from the vision it has of itself theologically. Instead of a growing diversity of fellowship amongst its members, people generally prefer to relate with others within ethnically homogeneous settings. As we saw in previous chapters, this may be a consequence of the entrenched ethnocentric tendencies that have historically shaped the ethnic components of the PCANZ. Even when congregations are diverse in their membership, they are internally organised in ways that promote ethnic similarity.

5 – Rethinking Our Fellowship

My ministry experiences at First Church retain their relevance. To relate more of that story, the issue regarding the possibility of separate communion services for the different ethnic groups was brought to the attention of the leadership group of the congregation as a way of seeking collective wisdom on the matter. Being a diverse group, it was not an easy topic to talk about openly and honestly. After much discussion there was an even split of opinion about whether to have separate communion services. We extended the discussion to those in the congregation who were interested to engage with the issue. Some thought that having separate services should not be seen so negatively since greater relevancy of worship content would also mean greater appreciation of it. Worshipping separately did not necessarily mean being divided as a church congregation. Others felt that the combined multilingual communion service was what made us unique as a congregation and that we were moving forwards in terms of closer relationships with each other. For them, retreating to separate services would be a backward step.

There was a desire for cultural relevancy regarding how they did things, yet also a yearning to preserve their unity. Wrestling with this issue created an awkward feeling for folk in sharing their sincere views for fear of affecting their long-time friendships with others. Some felt that if the communion services continued being multilingual they would find it increasingly difficult to attend. Similarly, others would possibly not attend because they felt that they and their culture were not appreciated. Doing things separately and in our own culturally familiar ways seemed easier, but living together differently was a real challenge.

As the minister, what should I do in such a situation? I may have my theological convictions about the Christian church and continue to encourage diverse fellowship together, but are they worth upholding if they split the congregation? Or, if I prevent people from walking away by providing for their religio-cultural needs, albeit separately, am I really serving faithfully in such a context with a clear conscience regarding my fundamental beliefs about the church? If nothing else, this story illustrates the high stakes of ethnic relations. This is important. In this chapter I would like to present areas of challenge and encouragement for people in congregations to consider how they might faithfully live out this theological imperative of unity in diversity. They are evaluating one's Christian identity, cross-cultural opportunities, learning from a pan-Pacific congregation model, and the challenge to congregations through sharing in Holy Communion.

Evaluating Christian Identity

From my congregation's experience of struggle around the issue of a multilingual Holy Communion service, we recognised that at the surface level there was the concern about language, but beneath that was a more fundamental issue: Christian identity and fellowship together as church. Evaluating our Christian identity is important because it can tell us something of what we know of ourselves and others as well as of our relationship with one another. To a great extent, our self-identities, our values, and our manner of giving meaning to experiences are developed in relationship to others.[269] Therefore, as individual Christians and as a community, we can come to understand and further appreciate our identity in Christ through the way we organise our life together. This understanding can also be shaped by the kind of Christians we relate with in terms of their ethno-cultural backgrounds.

From what we observed earlier, a Christological view of the church is grounded upon people's faith 'in Christ', making their Christian identity primary over other identity markers, including ethnic and cultural markers. The World Council of Churches (of which the PCANZ is a member) affirms this view by stating: "A crucial insight of the Christian faith is that all such identity markers are as nothing beside our new identity in Christ (Galatians 3:28): that no human identity markers, however positive and precious, can deny our primal belonging to Christ; and that no human distinctions, however pervasive and pernicious, can be allowed to separate us from our sisters and brothers in Christ."[270] A Christian identity has clear implications for the way Christians perceive others, as well as how they might engage with them.

Yet, the primacy of Christian identity does not negate or downplay people's distinctive characteristics.

> Christ calls us *past* our ethnicity, but not *out* of our ethnicity … The renewal of the New Humanity is not irrespective of differences of ethnicity and culture, but inclusive of such differences. The unity of the New Humanity is not "color blind." We are not collectively renewed as the New Humanity by superficially ignoring our differences of color and culture, but by profoundly appreciating our differences.[271]

Furthermore, contextualisation, as we previously observed, provides an opportunity for an engagement between gospel and culture so that through the transformation of a people's beliefs and practices, the gospel finds relevant expression regarding the group's cultural context. In commenting on this dialogue between gospel and culture, Anthony Gittins asserts that "Gospel must be 'translated' – carried over – into the lives and languages of actual people, a process that demands of its bearers familiarity both with the deep meanings of the gospel (text and context) and the deep needs and aspirations of people of particular cultures."[272] People have a right to understand and live out the gospel through their culture (language, customs, and traditions) in relevant ways that also affirm their Christian identity.

Despite appreciating cultural distinctiveness, however, Stevens reminds us that any differences between Christians should not be a categorising factor that determines their fellowship.

> The New Humanity is raceless only in the sense that ethnicity must never be the criteria for determining fellowship with God or with fellow believers. In other words, ethnic identity should no longer be a boundary marker for determining group identity, including the group identity of the local church.[273]

In this respect, Christian identity is not just an individual matter; it is also a communal matter that affects relationships within and between congregations.[274]

Although both gospel and culture are important for a meaningful and faithful expression of Christian identity, the challenge for individuals and communities is to engage in critical reflection about themselves, so as to keep a check on their Christian identity. In particular, they need to evaluate and recognise whether they emphasise one aspect over the other or whether a balance between gospel/faith and culture is maintained. One way of observing this is through assessing the religious practices of a group. If practices in a congregation encourage the ethnic and cultural homogeneity of its members, they most likely indicate a strong focus on the ethno-cultural aspect of their Christian identity.

Accentuating ethno-cultural aspirations makes obvious a Christian faith that desires to be lived out in a particular way among a particular people. It demonstrates a tendency to be distinct and therefore separate from others who are ethnically and culturally different. Acknowledging other Christians who are ethnically different is just that in terms of a living relationship in Christ. Although Christians may believe in the diversity of wider connections with others, placing an emphasis on the ethno-cultural aspect of their Christian identity can narrow down this belief to something that can only be exercised mainly through ethnic-specific connections. Within a homogeneous religious context, this kind of Christian identity can then be understood as the norm.[275] Such relations can reflect people's ethnocentric propensity and, in a way, also reveal a bias or prejudice for their own people. They may not necessarily discriminate against other Christians who are ethnically different from them, but they prefer confining their religious activity to settings in which people are like them.

There may also be a down-side to a Christian identity that focuses mainly on the faith aspect while ignoring the ethnic/cultural aspect. Those who are inclined to emphasise the universalising character of Christian faith tend to see this as paramount over ethnic and cultural issues. It means that matters essential to Christian faith become the only basis for connections and fellowship between Christians. As a consequence, Christians of different ethnic and cultural backgrounds can organise their religious life together as if such backgrounds are irrelevant or no longer necessary for the way they express their faith individually or collectively. But because the Christian faith has to be lived out through a cultural context, the question becomes 'how can this be done within an ethnically and culturally diverse congregation?' If the Christian faith is to be culturally relevant for people, through whose culture should it be expressed?

There must be some common cultural ground for fellowship within diverse congregations. An obvious need is for communication between people, and this will more likely be in the language of the majority culture of the society in which congregations are situated. In the New Zealand context, the English language reflects not only the population strength of people of European/Western descent but also of European/Western culture. We saw beforehand that within ethnically diverse congregations and combined worship services of pan-Pacific congregations, the English language and European traditions of liturgy are cultural media used to allow people of different ethnic and cultural backgrounds to fellowship together.

In essence, the dominant culture of society comes to be the culture through which most Christians express their faith. Because it can be perceived as being a neutral or common culture for all in the congregation, the dominant culture of society or of a particular group within a congregation can also be perceived as being a Christian culture. We saw this demonstrated in the Mosaic model. This is a congregation model of diversity in which the popular culture of society is promoted for negotiating a shared Christian identity over and against people's ethnic/cultural identity.

But if this Christian identity and culture is really that of the dominant culture, then it cannot really be neutral (if there is such a thing). The problem is that when a congregation promotes a Christian identity by emphasising matters of Christian faith through a culture that is perceived as being neutral, while excluding the ethno-cultural expressions of its respective members, it reflects uniformity to a dominant culture rather than the unity of the various cultures represented within it.

Our Trinitarian understanding of the unity in diversity of the Church is not uniformity. This kind of thinking does not value the ethnic/cultural background of Christians, as if such orientations cannot be perceived as Christian or enrich a Christian identity in any way. If the Mosaic model is really about negotiating a Christian identity and culture, it must surely include the ethno-cultural elements of its membership in order to truly demonstrate its diversity. A neutral Christian culture can also make Christian identity seem undistinctive and bland.

Keeping a check on Christian identity means evaluating the tendencies we have regarding the way we relate with others as people of God. It requires recognising the emphases we place between the cultural and faith aspects of our Christian identity, because it may also determine the kind of Christian company we keep, whether in ethnically homogeneous or diverse contexts. Evaluating one's Christian identity, context, and practices is important so that one can become more aware of and appreciate the wider scope of one's Christian community and relations, particularly with those who are ethnically and culturally different.

> The ability to make moral and ethical decisions based on contextual evaluation is the key to further development of a multicultural community. Contextual evaluation is the ability to analyze and evaluate situations relative to different cultural contexts. The end result of contextual evaluations is a judgment based on the relative goodness of the different cultural values involved but not conditioned by the situation in which judgement has to be made.[276]

Christian communities need to be aware of the cultural differences between themselves and others so that they are better able to relate more meaningfully and faithfully together. Ethnically diverse congregations may place an emphasis on the gospel dimension of a Christian identity, but to be faithful to their Christian identity they must also find ways, where practicable, of integrating the different cultural elements of their members as appropriate expressions of their faith. This can be hard work and even taxing upon people. Yet, such experiences, no matter how painful, can stretch people's mental, emotional, cultural, and spiritual capacity to accept and appreciate others who are different. When they can relate this action to Christ's love for the world, it can also enrich their faith and Christian identity.

Such an awareness of Christian identity challenges ethnically diverse congregations to explore better ways of not only appreciating the cultural variety of their members, but also allowing them into power-sharing arrangements. This requires congregation leaders and members to talk with and listen to one another while negotiating and working towards a shared vision of what their life together might look like. Practices such as these affirm what we previously noted in the works of Ammerman and Foster, who found that a shared church culture with an inclusive organisational identity could overcome the challenges and limitations rooted in ethnic and cultural differences. This can also promote a shared vision or hope for building caring relationships in diverse groups.

Homogeneous congregations, on the other hand, can highlight the cultural aspect of a Christian identity through the ethnic-specific representation of their members. This clearly distinguishes them from others. However, to be faithful to their Christian identity they are also challenged by the gospel aspect regarding the scope of their inclusiveness, particularly regarding those who are ethnically different from them. Although they may value their ethnic and cultural distinctiveness and choose to remain homogeneous, the gospel challenge to such a community context can include the extent to which they might consider cross-cultural opportunities with other communities.

People's Christian identity, in short, can be enhanced by interacting with other Christians who are both ethnically and culturally similar to and different from themselves. Admittedly, opportunities for this are more likely to occur within diverse congregations than homogeneous ones, but if a homogeneous congregation is truly serious about its Christian identity, then opportunities to interact with other congregations different from itself must be created or at the very least considered. When both contexts provide opportunities for this kind of interaction, they demonstrate the inclusive rather than exclusive character of their Christian identity.

In this regard, in examining the Apostle Paul's views about Christian identity and relations, Jason Goroncy argues that what Paul champions "is not that humanity has been liberated from religious boundaries in order to take up residence as a citizen of a secular, desacralised world, but rather that those baptised into Christ are now to live in the reality of Christ as both the boundary and centre of their existence, a boundary which includes all humanity in our cultural / ethnic / gendered / social / historical particularities."[277] This means that Christians and Christian communities must be mindful of their identity in terms of the scope with which they take account of and incorporate others in their life. How they engage with other Christians, particularly those who are ethnically different, will reveal how much they value their oneness in Christ.

Cross-Cultural Opportunities

All of this is a challenge to PCANZ congregations. Just because the PCANZ as a national body professes Christian unity in diversity and attempts to reflect this in its structures and processes, does this necessarily mean that its congregations must exemplify this at the local level? According to the Book of Order, there is nothing that offers guidance about ethnic relations for congregations. There seems to be a lack of any indication or reference that encourages congregations to consider ethnic or cultural diversity within and between them.

Yet the theological warrant for interaction in congregations between those similar to and distinct from each other is affirmed through our Trinitarian understanding of the church. We saw earlier that within the Trinity, each divine person does not exist exclusively in its own right, without the others, but operates perichoretically on the basis of an interrelatedness with each other. This model of the divine community must surely be considered as a basis for Christian congregations to try to live out the interconnectedness between distinct Christian groups. Such a rationale can be a starting point for encouraging ethnic diversity or cross-cultural engagements within and between congregations. If PCANZ congregations, most of which are ethnically homogeneous, remain isolated from others who are different, this does nothing to facilitate a broader understanding of their Christian identity.

To be faithful to this understanding, individuals and congregations must consider cross-cultural experiences and opportunities more seriously. Although attaining ethnic diversity in terms of membership and cross-cultural engagement is not the primary function of congregations, there are theological foundations and scope within PCANZ systems to do this.[278] If ethnic-specific congregations seek to enhance their homogeneity by limiting their engagement with Christians who are different from them, they may fall into the trap of what Philip Culbertson calls "egocentricity."

> Egocentricity, then, is the first enemy of cross-cultural sensitivity, though it is natural to human beings as breathing. Egocentricity is compounded by several other factors which work against cross-cultural sensitivity, including our own fear in the face of otherness that we will lose position, power, control, or even property; the threat of change and the attraction of the familiar; the baggage we carry from the past around all things personal, familial, and cultural; and our individual backlog of anger, suspicion and frustration over past encounters with otherness and difference. To work or live cross-culturally can be both frightening and bewildering, and yet it is to this arena of activity that the church is increasingly called.[279]

Culbertson affirms our earlier discussion on Christian identity and offers cross-cultural experiences as opportunities for congregation members to examine the perceptions they have of themselves and of others in the Body of Christ. Instead of simply focusing on the "otherness" of different Christians, cross-cultural experiences can enable Christians to appreciate a lived experience of the spiritual connections they have with others in Christ and the Trinity. These experiences might involve occasions for a meal in sharing ethnic food, cultural performances, learning a different language, sharing in a missional project, a camp, or a joint worship service together. Whatever the activity chosen for different groups to engage in, it can offer a practical expression of their unity in diversity.

There is no doubt that such cross-cultural interactions can be very challenging for people.[280] This is true for Christians as well. Although conflict can occur within homogeneous congregations, it can be heightened between different cultures within diverse congregations, and between ethnic-specific congregations that are different from each other. The difficulties and enormous effort put into cross-cultural relations is something we previously identified through the work of Emerson and Christerson. They argued that unless Christians accept and value such relations, they can feel marginalised and lose something of their religio-ethnic identity, compared to what they could receive in their own homogeneous congregation. Such feelings can weaken a sense of belonging between Christians and affect the congregation as a whole. Dietrich Bonhoeffer suggests that Christian communities can break down because they base their life together upon a "wish dream."[281] He explains:

> The serious Christian, set down for the first time in a Christian community, is likely to bring with him a very definite idea of what Christian life together should be and try to realize it. But God's grace speedily shatters such dreams. Just as surely as God desires to lead us to a knowledge of genuine Christian fellowship, so surely must we be overwhelmed by a great disillusionment with others, with Christians in general, and if we are fortunate, with ourselves. By sheer grace, God will not let us live even for a brief moment in a dream world.[282]

Bonhoeffer is arguing that the harmony we often envision about our congregational life together is not all that likely or even possible. But he suggests that Christians have no right or reason to be disillusioned when our experience of Christian fellowship does not meet our expectations. Since most congregations in the PCANZ are ethnically homogeneous, it seems that the "wish dream" or expectation is that they will live out their religiosity among those who are ethnically and culturally similar to them. Their "wish dream" anticipates familiarity. The unfamiliarity, effort, challenges, and conflicts that arise in cross-cultural interactions of diverse congregations can create this disillusionment.

However, differences between Christians do not have to be viewed solely in a negative light. Instead, they can become opportunities for Christians to better understand their life together as a community of God. To this effect, Bonhoeffer affirms that the illusions of Christians about their religious life need to be shattered.

> Only that fellowship which faces such disillusionment, with all its unhappy and ugly aspects, begins to be what it should be in God's sight, begins to grasp in faith the promise that is given to it ... A community which cannot bear and cannot survive such a crisis, which insists upon keeping its illusion when it should be shattered, permanently loses in that moment the promise of Christian community ... Every human wish dream that is injected into the Christian community is a hindrance to genuine community and

must be banished if genuine community is to survive. He who loves his dream of a community more than the community itself becomes a destroyer of the latter, even though his personal intentions may be ever so honest and earnest and sacrificial.[283]

Ironically, it is somehow in these very "unhappy" and "ugly" experiences of congregational life, particularly in cross-cultural interactions, where people's hopes and dreams are not met, that Christians can finally discover their life together. The challenges that Christians experience together are not only to be expected, but also something to be grateful for.[284] It is in struggles and pain with one another in congregational life that Christians encounter God's grace most completely. It is then that they can see Christ in the other whom they can truly call their neighbour. It is not because they necessarily like one another or agree with one another, but because their struggles can enable them to see more clearly what Christ has done for them. Where they were once estranged from God, through grace Christ reconciled them to God and to each other. In this way, they not only become more grateful for what Christ has done for them, but they can also have a greater appreciation of the unity in diversity of Christian community rather than their own ethnocentric views of it. As such, Bonhoeffer sees the Christian community as a gift from God whereby the challenges of cross-cultural interactions may "appear weak and trifling to us," but "may be great and glorious to God."[285]

Cross-cultural engagement between homogeneous congregations can allow them to understand other cultures better. A shared Christian identity, despite different cultural traditions, can enable a greater acceptance between Christian individuals and communities. Coming together to share something of each other's culture through joint activities such as those mentioned above (food, art, performance, or worship) provide opportunities for learning. What is learned about the "other" can contribute to a greater awareness of things that can help us to connect more authentically and lovingly with others who are different from us. We may be able to recognise something of ourselves in the other person. This is what van Beek, following David Augsburger, calls "interpathy."[286] Although applying this mainly within the cross-cultural pastoral counselling setting, interpathy can be extremely helpful for cross-cultural engagement between people of different congregations. In an interpathic relationship,

> people must see something of the other in themselves, and vice versa. This principle is at the heart of intercultural and interracial conflict and suspicion: One group is not able to see itself in the other. They see only something alien and therefore frightening. Identification and consequently interpathy is intentional. It means the willingness to be united in common experience.[287]

Experiencing interpathy in cross-cultural relations can reflect something of the perichoretic dynamic of the triune God. Although we may not fully understand how it happens, it portrays a sense of connecting, inter-weaving, and community-formation, all of which are important for congregations, even if these are only temporary experiences. Eric Law argues that such engagements need to be temporary because it is unrealistic to expect people to function outside their cultural boundaries all the time.[288] When they do engage, however, their temporary crossing over enables them to see the world and the church through very different eyes. Given the challenges of cross-cultural engagements, van Beek concludes that "it can be as dangerous and toilsome as it is enriching."[289]

If the PCANZ is serious about its diverse identity, then cross-cultural engagement has to happen in some way at the local level. Congregations do not exist in autonomous isolation from one another. Although they may have the freedom to develop in ethnically and culturally distinctive ways, congregations can be connected through local community links as well as through presbyteries, national ethnic bodies, and through representation at General Assembly. For example, a largely European congregation wanting to better accommodate ministry for some new Asian members could engage with a local Asian congregation or with the Asian Liaison person for advice and practical support. This could involve cross-cultural training for the leadership group of the congregation, or the provision of opportunities for a much wider group to explore studies about cultural protocols, customs, and language of a particular Asian group.

Structures are in place for congregations to engage with one another in ways that can affirm the distinctive religio-ethnic identity of some while encouraging diverse relations with others. In an interview for the PCANZ magazine *SPANZ*, Stuart Vogel encourages this view by asserting a shift from multiculturalism to cross-culturalism.

> The Church has been multicultural for 'quite some time,' Stuart explains, 'so it's timely for our churches to begin to engage in cross-cultural ministry together as well as focusing on ethnic ministries.' Stuart suggests the shift to cross-culturalism could gradually happen through churches intentionally interacting together during key events in worship, such as Easter and Christmas; and through joint outreach and mission both locally and overseas. 'We need to become more multi-lingual and flexible in the way we carry out our joint ministries through presbyteries and congregations.'[290]

What seems essential to Vogel's point is the intentionality of congregations regarding cross-cultural encounters. If congregations recognise and value their connections with others (who are different) in the presbytery, those connections have to be given life in practical ways rather than remain as good intentions. Congregations can have conversations with one another about what they might be able to do together. From time to time, a presbytery could order its business for meetings so that it acknowledges the diversity of representations within it and provides opportunities to hear about issues that are important to its ethnic minority groups. Such issues may not be major to the presbytery or the national church, but they go some way to intentionally giving a voice, face and place to these minority groups who deserve to be recognised within the PCANZ.

Our ecclesiology is one in which the church has a relational presence within the world. This is reflective of God's presence and work in both the church and world. The community of the Trinity is diverse and inter-relational. If this dynamic of God is the basis for the church as a whole, then it must also be applicable to the local congregation as well, because the local congregation is part of it. Congregations, whether predominantly European, Māori, Asian, Pacific Islander or ethnically diverse, should therefore intentionally seek to demonstrate this dynamic, where possible, within and between themselves. They must find ways of incorporating themselves into each other's life so that they can develop their common Christian identity and life together.

> The Spirit-filled community needs constant identity transformation in order to accept the diverse group 'others' who now are joining their ranks. The incorporation of the 'other' necessitates a 'dual identity transformation' that challenges the in-group to transform its own group identity. The Spirit is central to this process and both orchestrates inter-group contact and marks those who share a common identity.[291]

In this way, the various ethnic/cultural identities of people in a congregation live out a positive expression of their Christian identity and clearly manifest the unity in diversity of the church. Although the PCANZ is trying to demonstrate and encourage diversity from higher levels downward, I believe this identity can only be truly recognisable when occurring from the grassroots up.

Fellowshipping Differently:
A Pan-Pacific Congregation Model

Cross-cultural experiences can be both challenging and rewarding between ethnic-specific congregations, but they can be more so within diverse and pan-Pacific ones. Despite challenges that may reveal preferences for a homogeneous dynamic for groups, I would like to draw out some aspects from the pan-Pacific congregation model of ministry to present how cross-cultural engagements might encourage ethnic relations between people in congregations.

I have already described my experiences as a child growing up, and then as a minister serving within a pan-Pacific congregation, and the group dynamics within these congregations. To recap in brief, here the island groups organise themselves both collectively and separately. Collectively, they often have combined worship services and organisations (for example, elders group, choir, or youth group). Separately, they can also engage in the same activities. What is very obvious within pan-Pacific congregations is the space created for both shared and separate activities.

The use of community space can reveal the relationship dynamic of people within a congregation. For example, Kathleen Garces-Foley differentiates between churches that are space-sharing, multilingual, or pan-ethnic. Space-sharing churches are those that share or rent premises but have separate by-laws of incorporation, separate membership books, and separate finances. In some cases, the groups will have virtually no contact apart from procedural issues of space negotiated by the leadership.

Multilingual churches have often been established to serve the needs of immigrants who wanted worship in their native tongue. Unlike the space-sharing church, the multilingual church is a single entity that manages its diversity by holding separate services from the main language groups. While they may be one congregation, the ethnic groups within it tend to function separately from one another.

Pan-ethnic churches, on the other hand, have no institutionalised divisions along ethnic lines. The distinguishing features of pan-ethnic churches are a common language and "a shared racialised status" among people who identify with distinct ethnic groups.[292] Previously, we considered this understanding of a shared identity in Russell Jeung's research of pan-Asian congregations where Chinese, Koreans and Japanese saw themselves as Asian-Americans who preferred to do everything together in English.

What makes pan-Pacific congregations different from the ones described by Garces-Foley, as well as diverse congregations such as Mosaic, is that the ethnic groups within pan-Pacific congregations do things both collectively and separately. When working together, the respective groups express a shared Christian identity by their collaborative effort. This requires integration of the physical presence of people from each island group, including what they bring to their joint fellowship. In a combined worship service, English and their respective languages are presented through different elements of the liturgy (for example, prayers and hymns). Such congregations also encourage mixed representation and participation in various sub-groups of congregational life to establish a collective ownership of and responsibility for shared activities. Such practices, in turn, promote their shared Christian identity while upholding their cultural and faith values. In this respect, a pan-Pacific congregation model seeks to affirm positive experiences of cross-cultural encounters.

This kind of cross-cultural relationship requires space where cultural contributions can be made to reflect the unity in diversity of community life. Law points out that in order for diverse groups to engage meaningfully together, a congregation "must create a safe and non-judgmental environment."[293] No matter what the activity might be, groups within congregations must be open enough to provide room for sharing cultural perspectives and contributions toward a collective life, without fear of their contribution being perceived as inappropriate or devalued.

Creating space for cross-cultural interaction might seem like people giving up something to accommodate others. But a more positive approach sees it as encouraging people "to extend their boundary to consider the perspectives and experiences of others."[294] The space for doing things together in a pan-Pacific model is one in which people can add to, rather than take away from or deny, the religio-cultural gifts of different people in the community. The space for a cross-cultural life in a congregation is for the inclusion rather than the exclusion of others. Such a space and dynamic highlights the unity in diversity of a congregation.

Considering this aspect can go some way toward challenging people about how they can love their neighbour in light of the space they inhabit and the space they can share. In essence, the space for ethnic relations in a congregation is one of grace, through which individuals and groups can extend love or favour to each other as God has done for them.[295] In doing so, Christians can be faithful to the commandment of Jesus: "Just as I have loved you, you also should love one another" (John 13:34). A collective effort by different cultural elements coming together in a congregation can seem challenging and has the potential risk of conflict, but that is why grace is needed all the more.

The grace that is required to be exercised in a pan-Pacific model is not just for collective events, but also for when groups do things separately. There are some religious and cultural needs that can be met when people do things together, yet at other times they can be more meaningful when expressed within a particular cultural setting. For example, in the case of a combined worship service, despite using English as a common language of communication between the different island groups, as well as incorporating hymns in the language of the respective groups, it may be a challenge for those who do not have a good command of both English and other island languages which are not their own. Since cross-cultural interactions can require much more effort from people, having the space, time and means to do certain activities in culturally relevant and familiar ways can also provide a sense of cultural respite for ethnic groups. They do not have to work so hard at what they do because there is a familiarity that enables people to operate amongst their own people with more ease. Moreover, the time and space for ethnic-specific interests can strengthen the cultural aspect of a group's Christian identity. Therefore, the space that is important for doing things together between different ethnic groups is also important for doing things separately. Again, it is one given graciously by other groups for the benefit of the one seeking to fulfil its religio-cultural needs.

Yet combined events, such as worshipping together, can help broaden people's knowledge of others who are different. When Christians genuinely value their brother or sister in Christ and make efforts to appreciate their cultural and religious perspectives, this can enrich the Christian identity of those involved. The church space they share, though fixed in a physical and structural sense, becomes figuratively malleable in terms of the different peoples that occupy it, as well as the different ways they use it. As such, it portrays a different sense of identity for what the space represents.

Commenting on the revitalisation of Jewish conceptions of sacred and profane space, Joseph Hellerman suggests that a "fixed sacred space becomes a fluid sacred space as the locus of God's dwelling place moves from a permanent geo-political location (the Jerusalem temple) to the 'mobile and portable' *ekklesia* of God."[296] Within pan-Pacific congregations, people will often adjust their perceptions of and behaviour with others as their religious environment changes – for example, as they move between diverse and homogeneous settings in their church building. This movement demonstrates awareness of the people and relations present in the space that is shared, and Christians accordingly adjust the way they engage together. This can help to keep the awareness of their Christian unity in diversity before them.

The pan-Pacific model does require much effort, patience, tolerance, and wisdom, but it can also clearly exhibit the intentionality of building a Christian community based upon the complex yet wonderful dynamic of the community of the triune God. Although it necessitates people of different cultural backgrounds finding ways of working together, the relationships within such a model do not force people to change to be something they are not or to deny who they are. This is a model of congregation life that Bonhoeffer affirms:

> I must release the other person from every attempt of mine to regulate, coerce, and dominate him with my love. The other person needs to retain his independence of me; to be loved for what he is.[297]

Instead, the pan-Pacific model of ministry can help people realise what it means to be a community of grace. As Bonhoeffer asserts, such a community requires people to be gracious enough to accept and love others as they are just as Christ has done for them. Inclusive of encouraging awareness of Christian identity, this model of ministry also develops a greater appreciation of an ecclesiology of unity in diversity.

Challenged by Holy Communion

There must be some tangible act or form of fellowship that consistently makes obvious the unity in diversity of the church at the local congregation level. I believe the fellowship of Holy Communion in a congregation is a witness to this dynamic because, as a sacrament, it is also a central practice of the church. It is a sacrament practiced most often at the congregational level, within both ethnically homogeneous and diverse congregations. Further theological exploration of this core expression of congregational life is critical for our understanding of ethnic relations in a Christian community. Examining the theology and practice of Holy Communion will show how it can encourage unity and diversity within a congregation as well as safeguard against ethnocentric practices that have the potential for division. Moreover, it will help to inform a constructive response to the challenging scenario we saw at First Church.

The sacrament of Holy Communion is the sharing of bread and wine that symbolises the body and blood of Christ. It is also known as the Lord's Supper, the Lord's Table, or Eucharist. The event of Holy Communion is narrated in the Gospels (Matthew 26:26-29; Mark 14:22-26; Luke 22:14-23), and the tradition is also passed on by the Apostle Paul in 1 Corinthians 11:23-26.

Holy Communion is an expression of the church's faith in the salvific death and resurrection of Christ. If the other sacrament of the PCANZ, baptism, signifies God's love that welcomes a person into the new Christian community, then Holy Communion marks God's continued sharing of life and love that gives strength to the new community.

Sacraments have four basic functions: to convey grace, strengthen faith, enhance unity and commitment within the church, and reassure us of God's promises toward us.[298] These functions are not merely for the sake of an individual but, rather, for the sake of the Christian community. For example, if grace is understood as "an objective relation of undeserved favour by a superior to an inferior," as in the case of divine grace toward humankind, then this implies relations between those who are different.[299] We have seen earlier that this is a favourable space that enables a connection between parties who are separated by difference. Grace provides the time and space for differences to be worked out together. Just as humanity is reconciled to God through the grace of Christ, so too are Christians, regardless of their distinctive characteristics, reconciled to one another in the same grace. The diverse fellowship together of Christians in Holy Communion is a concrete expression of Christ's grace that is lived out in human relations.

The term "Holy Communion" implies a common unity in Christ and with each other in the church. Therefore, participation in Holy Communion represents a continuing public declaration of loyalty to the church and loyalty to each other in the church. This is a loyalty and commitment that crosses ethnic and cultural lines between Christians. For Migliore, those who partake of this meal "are made one community in Christ."[300] It is a sacrament and fellowship that symbolises not only what the church believes, but also what it is – the body of Christ that is diverse in its parts, yet united.

If this is so, sharing in Holy Communion is a practice that seeks to be inclusive of all in the church, irrespective of distinctive characteristics. As a public, joyful, hopeful meal, Holy Communion is a foretaste of a new humanity in Christ.[301] Anything contrary to this creates barriers that limit people from fully participating in this new humanity and is thus a sign of unfaithfulness to our calling to open and inclusive fellowship in the body of Christ. In light of this, Christians cannot, on the one hand, eat and drink at the Lord's Table "where all are welcome and none goes hungry or thirsty," but then "continue to condone any form of discrimination or any social or economic policy that results in hunger or other forms of deprivation."[302] This view makes it clear that a congregation that celebrates Holy Communion while organising its fellowship in ways that affirm some while excluding others, even on the basis of ethnic and cultural differentiations, is not being consistent with what it believes regarding the sacrament and regarding itself as the church.

In some ways, a situation like this is not new; it reflects a tension present in one of the earliest Christian communities. Greek-speaking Jewish Christians who had fled persecutions in Jerusalem eventually reached Antioch, where they introduced the Christian message to Gentiles (Acts 11:19-20).[303] This diversity gave rise to the issue of the admission of Gentiles into the Christian community with respect to Jewish observances (Acts 15; Galatians 2). Although Gentile admission was accepted in principle (Acts 15:13-29; Galatians 2: 7-10), in practice it was very difficult, particularly with regard to their fellowship meals (Galatians 2:11-14).

Some scholars suggest that under such pressure the church remained diverse, although Jewish and Gentile Christians might have formed "separate fellowships, presumably meeting in different houses."[304] David Sim goes further to argue that the church in Antioch eventually reverted to a Jewish Christian character.[305] These situations do not reflect the spirit of unity in diversity of the Christian community. The Christian message that initially brought different cultures together must be the same message that is symbolically represented in the sacrament of Holy Communion.

As a sacrament that expresses the connectedness of the divine and humanity, as well as the connectedness of people within humanity, Holy Communion speaks directly to the unity in diversity of both the Church and God. According to Migliore, when its function is fulfilled as a sacrament, Holy Communion is a portrayal of the "interconnection and interdependence of personal, communal, and cosmic salvation."[306] If this is true, then the fellowship of Holy Communion is one that must move towards this fulfilment by enacting it amongst those who participate.

As an expression of God's saving grace in the world, this understanding of Holy Communion provides a broader view of the Christian community to include all kinds of people. For congregation members this view cannot be exclusively limited to those who are ethnically similar when celebrating the sacrament. Those who are used to having Holy Communion within an ethnically homogeneous context might gain a greater appreciation of God's saving grace when sharing the sacrament with other Christians who are ethnically different from them. It can be a reminder to them of how God's love creates and sustains a much broader and diverse Christian community.

There is nothing wrong with an ethnically homogeneous congregation celebrating Holy Communion since it has a "spiritual" fellowship with the wider diverse church. But the unity in diversity of the church to which the sacrament points will challenge such a congregation regarding how it can faithfully live this out at the local level if diversity continues not to be evident in its membership. Ministers and parishioners who talk about the unity in diversity of the church in terms of Holy Communion, while continuing with practices that encourage a congregation's homogeneity or seriously limiting cross-cultural engagements with other Christians, can make such talk seem very shallow and hypocritical. A Christian congregation that celebrates the sacrament of Holy Communion and values its significance would have to rethink how open it really is regarding diversity, so that it can faithfully demonstrate what it stands for as the church.

Since Holy Communion is a sacrament in which Christians continually participate, it provides the opportunity for ongoing challenges to congregations about their openness toward others. Moltmann sees the regular fellowship of Holy Communion as the "eschatological sign of being on the way."[307] It is an ongoing reminder to people of their links to a Christian community that is developing in ways that serve God's ultimate purpose of the reconciliation of all creation to God. The links are also much broader and extend the connection to other levels of the church. The catholicity of the church does not mean anything else but the wholeness and totality of the body of Christ, exactly as it is portrayed in the community that celebrates Holy Communion.[308] To understand a congregation in this way implies that, by participating in Holy Communion, the congregation's fellowship is reflective of the unity in diversity of the whole church. This must surely include ethnic and cultural diversity amongst members in the congregation.

Holy Communion is not just for some in the church, it is for all. This is because Christ who was sent into the world and who loved it and died for it is the same Christ who instituted Holy Communion. It is the Lord's Supper and not something organised by a church or denomination. As Moltmann puts it, the fellowship of Holy Communion is grounded upon the openness of Christ's invitation to the world.

> If a church were to limit the openness of his invitation of its own accord, it would be turning the Lord's Supper into the church's supper and putting its own fellowship at the centre…The theological doctrine of the Lord's Supper must consequently not be allowed to exercise any controversial theological function through which Christians are separated from Christians. If it represents the supper as being the supper of the Lord, then it is setting itself in the sphere of interest of his open invitation and is giving effect to that invitation… Just as the Lord's supper is a sign of fellowship and not of division, so the corresponding theology will have to present what is in common and not what divides.[309]

The fellowship of Holy Communion cannot be limited in any sense. Since Christ died for the reconciliation of the world, the world is invited into reconciliation in the act of Communion. The openness of the crucified Lord's invitation to his supper and his fellowship reaches beyond the boundaries of different denominations. This must surely include individuals or people groups in the church with distinctive ethnic and cultural identities. Although we have noted that homogeneous congregations may be valid as Christian communities in their own right, the meaning of inclusion and diversity associated with the celebration of Holy Communion which they celebrate must, again, surely confront them about how limiting their homogeneous practices might be. It is not the openness of Christ's invitation but, rather, the restrictive measures of churches that have to be justified before Christ.[310]

Just as our ecclesiology includes a Trinitarian perspective that is conducive to unity in diversity, so too does a Trinitarian understanding of Holy Communion. It is a thanksgiving to God the Father for everything made in creation; to the Holy Spirit, as the power of the Kingdom, who gives a foretaste of the new creation in the feast; and to Christ, who reconciles the world to God.[311] The divine relationship of the triune God understood and signified in Holy Communion again portrays the unity in diversity of the church. This aspect reiterates Moltmann's view of how this dynamic must be reflected in the communities that celebrate Holy Communion.

> Because the fellowship of the table unites believers with the triune God through Christ, it also causes men to unite with one another in messianic fellowship… The open invitation of the crucified one to his supper is what fundamentally overcomes all tendencies towards alienation, separation and segregation. For through giving himself up to death for the fellowship of men with God and with one another, the godless and inhuman divisions and enmities between races, nations, civilizations and classes are overcome. Churches which permit these deadly divisions in themselves are making the cross of Christ a mockery. [312]

There is no room, then, for practices in congregations that potentially divide people through the pursuit of ethnocentric interests. Although such interests may make Christian faith feel more meaningful, as well as helping various communities to maintain their distinctive ethnic and cultural character, they also have the capacity to separate or isolate communities. Church practises that discourage diversity through cross-cultural engagement between Christian groups while instead promoting their homogeneity through isolation from each other are incoherent with our theological understanding of church and Holy Communion. The "mockery" that Moltmann alludes to is the fact that ethnocentric practices that keep Christians apart are contrary to the cross of Christ, which reconciles them to each other and to God.

Similarly, there is a dichotomy between the policies and vision of the PCANZ (through its Book of Order and Kupu Whakapono) that envisions the unity in diversity of its members and the ethnocentric practices of its congregations that segregate them. The latter raises the issue of the agency and relationship of individual congregations and the connectional life of the Church. Despite congregations developing in ethnic-specific ways, Holy Communion, like the cross of Christ, is a sign and constant reminder to them of diverse Christian connections. As a sign of grace also, celebrating Holy Communion provides the space for homogeneous congregations to change so that they begin to reflect and live out the unity in diversity which the sacrament represents.

Some congregations, of course, are ethnically homogeneous by default because they reflect the population in which they are located. They may have no choice but to organise themselves within their context, while still claiming their links to the wider diverse church through their Christian identity and celebration of Holy Communion. But we noted that most PCANZ congregations were ethnically homogeneous despite being located in geographical areas with broader ethnic representations. Celebrating Holy Communion in these congregations, while clearly confining their Christian fellowship to their own kind, is inconsistent with what Holy Communion symbolises. Claiming that a "spiritual" relationship with other Christians and congregations in the wider church is sufficient is a very weak substitute for an intentional and active relationship of belonging in the Body of Christ with others who are different. This cannot be used as an excuse that encourages homogeneity in congregations. A faithful ecclesiology encourages diversity in local congregations.

Conclusion

Changes to our life as individual Christians and as communities requires a rethinking of ourselves. It challenges us about the reality of the aspects of our life that we either emphasise or try to balance in demonstrating our Christian identity. Stressing ethno-cultural aspects can produce homogeneity in our fellowship, while simply highlighting a faith aspect without ethno-cultural content can be a sign of depreciating the value of different people and what they can contribute to the fellowship. Much harder, though just as important, is the intentional incorporation of both these aspects so that not only are the relations among and between church members enriched, so too is the composition of a congregation. Taking seriously the ecclesiology of unity in diversity means having a good look again at our practices and the ideas that inform them to see whether they are consistent with our understanding of God and God's church. In this way we can affirm the things we do well and acknowledge blind spots of prejudice and fear that have shaped us. This is good because we begin from a point of honesty. It may be hard to accept what we see in the mirror, but if there is to be any change in the life of a congregation, it must begin with the person whose reflection it is in the mirror.

While ethno-cultural homogeneity can bring familiarity, stability, and comfort for people in a congregation, the tension and often painful experiences of diversity can remind its members that they are alive. That is what cross-cultural encounters can bring. Cultures are not static in that they do not remain unchanged. Numerical and spiritual growth can also include an emerging cultural awareness of parishioners and clergy. These are learning opportunities that enable people in congregations to mature in their understanding and appreciation of others (and of themselves) rather than becoming stuck or stunted because of ignorance. The latter might be used as an excuse for inactivity, but not for the overall ill health of a congregation's life. A congregation should not have to tear apart or die because of ethno-cultural tensions between its members. The struggles and learning from cross-cultural encounters can become an exercise of their Christian faith to make individuals and communities stronger, not weaker.

Such dynamics in cross-cultural experiences are very evident in pan-Pacific congregations. In this type of congregation model different groups have to negotiate and share their time, space, and activities. Ethnic relations, then, become an exercise of how people groups can be more accepting of and gracious to one another in the same place. For Pacific Islanders, this is, in essence, a core cultural value of respect – for one's self and for others. It enables different groups to express their religiosity in culturally appropriate ways both separately and corporately. In this congregation model respect is the practice of caring reciprocation that seeks the wellbeing of groups and for the congregation as a whole. Although this model can be very testing for a diverse congregation, it will reveal the extent to which different peoples within them are prepared to share their life together.

I believe Holy Communion is the test of such an extent. As a sacrament, the elements and words used in association with them clearly endorse what it means to be the church. Ministers and parishioners who partake of this sacrament cannot avoid the deafening call to the unity in diversity of the Body of Christ. Yet, the vast majority of ethnically homogeneous congregations suggest that they do not hear it. Perhaps what they hear, accept, and embrace instead is the message of unity. Diversity, for whatever reason, does not register on their theological radar. Maybe congregations should reconsider using different languages in the Communion liturgy, like at First Church, with the hope that people will pay attention, even if by upsetting some.

Conclusion

What we believe of ourselves to being the church and the reality of that in our congregations can be two very different things. Often our Christian fellowship tends to be shaped more by our ethno-cultural preferences rather than by our theological convictions. This has clearly been revealed in my exploration of PCANZ congregations. People tend to be involved with congregations along ethnic and cultural lines. They may express preferences such as a particular style of worship, ministry, or location, but in terms of a congregation to call 'home', most folk are also profoundly swayed by ethnic and cultural influences.

To recap my observations, the vast majority of PCANZ congregations were ethnically homogeneous, while few were ethnically diverse. Whatever the preferences for the type of congregation people want to belong to, such preferences tend to be lived out within a particular ethnic and cultural framework of the majority membership of a congregation. This observation reflects much of the research done on religious communities in the United States by the likes of Emerson and Chaves and confirms the homogeneity of different groups in the New Zealand context.

Similarly, although many congregations are located in areas of diversifying populations, these congregations are mostly homogeneous. This reveals that while people may experience greater cross-cultural diversity in the wider society where they are located, their experiences of diverse ethnic relations in their congregations are very limited. Perhaps this is a consequence of the voluntary nature of churches, as opposed to the necessary or compulsory character of other institutions such as schools and workplaces, where people have to work alongside and engage with those who are ethnically different.

Yet some settings did reflect diversity in PCANZ congregations. For example, the population in the Auckland region had greater ethnic diversity than other places in New Zealand, and this was mirrored in its presbytery having the highest number of diverse congregations compared to the other presbyteries. Even so, there was still a higher representation of homogeneous congregations in its bounds. This suggests that, given a choice, parishioners are prepared to commute within their presbytery area, if necessary, in order to fellowship in congregations that also affirm their ethnic and cultural identity.

Again, these features point to the reality that people are inclined to express their religiosity in quite homogeneous ways. It is not surprising, then, that most congregations were represented mainly by Europeans *or* Māori *or* Asians *or* Pacific Islanders. Subsequently, the ethnic representation of subgroups within the congregation, such as the leadership group, also reflected the homogeneity of the congregation as a whole.

I also witnessed that congregations were more inclined to have clergy who were ethnically matched with the largest ethnic group within them. Even if there were multiple ministers in a congregation, each minister tended to be ethnically matched with at least one group in the congregation. This was particularly the case for pan-Pacific congregations. What this exposes, is that although clergy are trained in the theology and practices of church ministry extended to all in the PCANZ, they are in fact inclined to confine their ministry to congregations that affirm ethnic ties.

Clergy who disagreed or who denied a bias of ministry towards their own ethnic group usually put it down to their sense of call by God, or to how they perceived their ability or suitability to work in a particular congregation. Without questioning their spiritual convictions, the obvious homogeneity of the religious communities in which they operate suggests a form of colour-blindness on their part. They do not recognise prejudices because their ethnic-specific context is the norm for them. However, not all clergy are like this. There are ministers who serve within congregations as ethnic minorities, but these cases are undoubtedly exceptions to most others. Clergy who serve as ethnic minorities in their congregations demonstrate that they can learn new skills (including language and cultural protocols), no matter how difficult, to help them work more effectively across cultures. Apart from discerning God's calling for them, ministers are in a position, because of their theological training, to give witness to and to develop diversity in congregations.

Worship services are a good predictor of ethnic relations. They are usually conducted in the language of the predominant ethnic group of a congregation. As such, the ethnic representation of worshippers is inclined to mirror the predominant group in the congregation. In diverse and pan-Pacific congregations, the English language is used as a common language to enable different groups to participate in worship together. This was a context in which ethnic diversity was most noticeable. However, when a congregation had multiple services, each conducted in the vernacular of its respective ethnic groups, such services leaned towards being ethnic-specific in terms of those who attended them. Within PCANZ congregations, when given a choice for the kind of worship service parishioners can attend, they often choose the one that affirms their ethnic and cultural needs as well as their religious ones.

There is no doubt that the PCANZ as a whole is diverse, with many ethnicities represented within it. This diversity is also worked out in the representative and consultative processes of various committees at national and regional levels. But what we have seen so far indicates that, on the ground, ethnic and cultural identities are represented in ways that are generally homogeneous. Such contexts provide familiarity, comfort, and ease. The low number of ethnically diverse congregations shows that people may find it hard to envision and appreciate a Christian identity over and above an ethnic and cultural identity. It is much harder still to live out that Christian identity in practice.

The homogeneity of PCANZ congregations is understandable considering the ethnocentric ways in which Presbyterianism developed historically amongst Europeans, Māori, Asians, and Pacific Islanders in New Zealand. It reflects the consequences of earlier missionary practices that used indigenous Christians to evangelise their own people, establish congregations for them, and eventually serve as religious leaders within them.

Although Presbyterianism has, by and large, kept its Scottish character and forms, and has expected the other ethnic components to adapt themselves accordingly, these components have become agents of cultural change themselves. By upholding their ethno-cultural identity as a lens through which to shine the light of the Christian gospel, they have respectively developed in ways portraying very distinctive identities within the PCANZ. The sense of distance or separateness, the lack of cross-cultural interaction between the congregations of these ethnic components, and their selective operations among their own kind further contribute to the growing homogeneity of their congregations.

Perhaps PCANZ congregations today are feeling the effects of the lack of effort put into encouraging the integration of its ethnic components. Individuals or representatives from various groups may work together as a sign of the unity in diversity of the PCANZ at higher levels, but at the local level, except for diverse and pan-Pacific congregations, there seems to be very little to show for any commitment to this dynamic within and between congregations.

Congregations cannot expect to remain unaffected by the call to be agents of transformation in a changing world. As congregations seek to fulfil their Christian mission of giving witness to the good news of Jesus Christ within their own local context, they must consider how that mission shapes them as well. I have already presented a Christological and Trinitarian ecclesiology that strongly argues for the unity in diversity of the church. This must, at some point, be manifested in the local congregation. Ethnic and cultural diversity is emerging in different public sectors such as education and health. Yet church congregations continue to be largely homogeneous. Partly this is because of the voluntary nature of the church. But if congregations want to be truly faithful to what is fundamental about the Christian church, then diversity must eventually develop. It will happen by aligning the ethnic, cultural, and spiritual needs and identity of people to that of the Christian identity that is lived out in the community of the triune God.

Change is not easy for congregations, especially for those who have long and proud histories and traditions. But it is the nature of the church to progress since it is on an eschatological journey. Presbyterianism has developed in homogeneous ways amongst its four main ethnic components for most of its time in New Zealand, but this is changing slowly. It is not a matter of when, but how.

The aspiration of unity in diversity of the PCANZ at its higher levels has the opportunity to permeate all its congregations. It does not have to be limited to representation by individuals of different groups. The PCANZ has the theology (which can also help it to explore practices relevant to the New Zealand context), structures and governance to make this new life possible within its congregations at the local level. Although its Book of Order does not say much about ethnic relations at the congregational level, that should not prevent PCANZ congregations from putting into practice what they believe of themselves overall. Presbyterians cannot confess in the *Kupu Whakapono* that "in Christ *he iwi kotahi tatou* [we are one people], witnesses to God's love in word and action, servants of reconciliation" while congregating in ways that clearly set its members apart by ethnic and cultural boundaries. It requires courage and humility by confessors to explore how these words can enable ethnic unity in diversity to be put into action.

Often when congregations have the determination and patience to become authentically diverse they will overcome the challenges highlighted in this exploration. Finding a balance between meeting the ethnic and cultural needs of members and also being faithful to their ecclesiology is difficult. Tensions can cause the differences between ethnic groups to flare up with such intensity that they can burn bridges that once connected them. These are bridges that enable cross-cultural experiences between different peoples rather than experiences that encourage ethnic homogeneity within people groups.[313]

Yet the PCANZ emblem of the burning bush that was not consumed is a sign of hope. The tensions and conflicts are reminders of the cost of following Jesus, who set the example of openness and inclusion of others. "For the closer we come to each other, the more painful is the experience that we are not yet in full communion."[314] The difficulties inherent in this commitment become the challenge to accept and work with those perhaps seen as too different to understand, or even an enemy, so that we can love one another as they have been loved by Christ.

If there is a congregation on fire because of ethnic and cultural tensions, then it is a sign not so much of the incompatibility of its members, but rather the incompatibility of their practices with the belief of the church that embraces all believers. Just as God spoke through the burning bush to begin the process of setting the Israelites free from slavery in Egypt, the burning congregation has an opportunity to hear God speak freedom for itself, freedom from the slavery of narrow-mindedness, and freedom from the oppressive nature of control. Congregations need to be set free from the attitude that some groups have more rights than others in being the church. This challenge hits at the very heart of the question, 'who is really the church?'

Burning congregations do not have to be consumed by ethnic flames. Instead, they can be a light radiating the glory of Christ's redeeming and reconciliatory work to an often-divided church and world. Such congregations can be a light: not only are they a beacon of hope for other congregations in a storm of ethnic relations, but their light can also provide Christian warmth exemplified through the "unity of the Spirit in the bond of peace" (Ephesians 4:3). Diverse congregations can show the way in which open acceptance, sincere appreciation of distinctions between peoples, and an abundance of patience can bear fruit. This requires God's grace to give us the time and space to grow and learn together. Duane Elmer puts it succinctly when he says, "I need to learn to adapt to the cultural lens of the local people. That would require not setting my lens aside, but adding theirs to mine."[315] There is a great cost entailed in working in such congregations, but it is worth the effort because they can be embraced as a gift from God to be celebrated, rather than a burden that weighs them down. They are the foretaste of God's Kingdom on earth that will be realised in the completion of its coming.

Finally, this is a telling of my own story. It reflects my journey in church ministry within both a pan-Pacific and a diverse congregation. In them I have seen the pain and joy, the ugliness and beauty, the despair and satisfaction, and the losses and victories of ethnic relations in the body of Christ. My exploration has challenged me to look honestly at myself in the mirror of Christ, to acknowledge my own preferences for those who are the same as me, and to recognise the fears, lack of understanding, and value of those who are different.

If PCANZ congregations are to be truly faithful to what they believe and confess, they can begin by looking at themselves in the mirror as well. I have tried to portray an honest picture of what I think the PCANZ looks like at different levels, particularly at the congregational level. There are some things that look promising and there are others that need transformation. We may not always get things right in Christian congregations, but in Christ God has put us together with one another, with some who are similar to us, and with others who are different. Our experiences together can involve the best of times as well as the worst. But in these experiences, we can discover something much more about the kind of community God is creating by grace through us and often in spite of us. Distinctive colours and patterns are beautiful and interesting in themselves and on their own, but when put together creatively, carefully, and lovingly they can become a masterpiece to behold. The image I see is colourful flames reminding me that the different people in the Church and in my congregation, including me, are God's people and are therefore my people too.

Bibliography

Arbuckle, Gerald A., SM. *Earthing the Gospel: An Inculturation Handbook for Pastoral Workers*. London: Geoffrey Chapman, 1990.

Alumkal, A. "Being Korean, Being Christian: Particularism and Universalism in a Second-generation Congregation." In *Korean Americans and their Religions: Pilgrims and Missionaries from a Different Shore*, ed. H. Y. Kwon, K. C. Kim, and R. S. Warner, 181-192. University Park, PA: Pennsylvania State University, 2001.

Ammerman, Nancy T. *Congregations and Community*. New Brunswick, NJ: Rutgers University Press, 1997.

Ammerman, Nancy T., Jackson W. Carroll, Carl S. Dudley, and William McKinney, eds. *Studying Congregations: A New Handbook*. Nashville, TN: Abingdon Press, 1998.

Augsburger, David. *Conflict Mediation Across Cultures: Pathways and Patterns*. Louisville, KY: Westminster John Knox Press, 1995.

— *Pastoral Counseling Across Cultures*. Louisville KY: Westminster John Knox Press, 1986.

Barber, Laurie. "The Expanding Frontier (1901-1930)." In *Presbyterians in Aotearoa, 1840-1990*, ed. Dennis McEldowney, 74-102. Wellington: Presbyterian Church of New Zealand, 1990.

Barclay, John M. G. "Universalism and Particularism: Twin Components of both Judaism and Early Christianity." In *A Vision for the Church: Studies in Early Christian Ecclesiology in Honour of J. P. M. Sweet*, ed. Markus Bockmuehl and Michael B. Thompson, 207-224. Edinburgh: T&T Clark, 1997.

Barker, John. "An Outpost in Papua: Anglican Missionaries and Melanesian Teachers among the Maisin, 1902-1934." In *Studies in Christian Mission* 31, ed. Marc R. Spindler, 79-106. Leiden: Brill Academic Publishers, 2005.

Beaver, R. Pierce. "The History of Mission Strategy." In *Perspectives on the World Christian Movement*, 3rd ed., ed. Ralph D. Winter and Steven C. Hawthorne, 241-252. Pasadena, CA: William Carey Library, 1981.

Best, Ernest. *Ephesians*. International Critical Commentary. Edinburgh: T&T Clark, 1998.

Blomberg, Craig L. "The Authenticity and Significance of Jesus' Table Fellowship with Sinners." In *Key Events in the Life of the Historical Jesus*, ed. Darrell L. Block and Robert L. Webb, 215-250. Tübingen: Morh Siebeck, 2009.

Bolaffi, Guido, Raffaele Bracalenti, Peter Braham, and Sandro Gindro, eds. *Dictionary of Race, Ethnicity and Culture*. London: Sage Publications, 2003.

Bonhoeffer, Dietrich. *Life Together*. Translated from the 5th edition by John W. Doberstein. London: SCM Press, 1954.

Borg, Marcus J., and John Dominic Crossan. *The First Paul: Reclaiming the Radical Visionary behind the Church's Conservative Icon*. New York: HarperOne, 2009.

Brändle, Rudolf, and Ekkehard W. Stegemann. "The Formation of the First 'Christian Congregations' in Rome in the Context of the Jewish Congregations." In *Judaism and Christianity in First-Century Rome*, ed. Karl P. Donfried and Peter Richardson, 117-127. Grand Rapids, MI: William B. Eerdmans, 1998.

Branson, Mark Lau, and Juan F. Martinez. *Churches, Cultures and Leadership: A Practical Theology of Congregations and Ethnicities*. Downers Grove, IL: InterVarsity Press, 2011.

Brislin, Richard W., Kenneth Cushner, Craig Cherrie and Mahealani Yong. *Intercultural Interactions: A Practical Guide*. Vol. 9, Cross-Cultural Research and Methodology Series. Beverly Hills, CA: Sage, 1986.

Brock, Peggy. "Setting the Record Straight: New Christians and Mission Christianity." In *Studies in Christian Missions* 31, ed. Marc R. Spindler, 107-128. Leiden: Brill Academic Publishers, 2005.

Brown, Raymond E. *The Gospel According to John (xiii-xxi)*. The Anchor Bible Commentary. New York: Doubleday and Company, 1970.

Brueggemann, Walter. "The Prophet as a Destabilizing Presence." In *The Pastor as Prophet*, ed. Earl E. Shelp and Ronald H. Sunderland, 49-77. New York: Pilgrim Press, 1985.

Bruner, Frederick Dale. *The Gospel of John: A Commentary*. Grand Rapids, MI: William B. Eerdmans, 2012.

Butcher, Andrew and George Wieland, "Go from your Country: Missiological Reflections on Asian Christians in New Zealand." *Stimulus* 18, no. 1 (February 2010): 2-8.

Campbell, William S. "The Addressees of Paul's Letter to the Romans: Assemblies of God in House Churches and Synagogues." In *Between Gospel and Election*, ed. Florian Wilk and J. Ross Wagner, with assistance of Frank Schleritt. Wissenschaftliche Untersuchungen zum Neuen Testament 257, 171-196. Tübingen: Morh Siebeck, 2010.

Carter, Warren. "Matthew's People." In *Christian Origins: A People's History of Christianity*, ed. Richard A. Horsley, 138-161. Minneapolis, MN: Fortress Press, 2005.

Census of Population and Dwellings 2006, New Zealand. Wellington: Statistics New Zealand, 2006.

Chai, Karen. "Competing for the Second Generation: English-language Ministry in a Korean Protestant Church." In *Gatherings in Diaspora: Religious Communities and the New Immigration*, ed. R. Stephen Warner and Judith G. Wittner, 295-331. Philadelphia: Temple University Press, 1998.

Challis, Robert L. *Pacific Islanders in New Zealand*. Bulletin for Schools. Wellington: Schools Publication Branch, Department of Education, 1970.

— *Social Problems of Non-Māori Polynesians in New Zealand*. Technical Paper no. 41. Sydney: South Pacific Commission, 1953.

Chambers, Jim Bernard. *A Peculiar People: Congregationalism in New Zealand 1840-1984 including the Congregational Union of New Zealand 1884-1984*. Levin: Congregational Union of New Zealand, 1984.

Chaves, Mark. *National Congregations Study*. Tucson, AZ: Department of Sociology, University of Arizona, 1999.

Chinese Presbyterian Church of Dunedin. Annual Report, 1960. Dunedin: PCANZ Archives.

Christerson, B., B. K. L. Edwards, and M. O. Emerson. *Against All Odds: The Struggle for Racial Integration in Religious Organizations*. New York: New York University Press, 2005.

Clark, Gordon H. *What Do Presbyterians Believe? The Westminster Confession: Yesterday and Today*. Philadelphia: The Presbyterian Reformed Publishing Co., 1965.

Crawford, Horace John. *A Noble Record: One Hundred Years of Presbyterian Church Government in Auckland, 1856-1956*. Auckland: Presbyterian Church of New Zealand, 1956.

Croucher, Rowland. "Church Growth and Pastoral Stress." In *John Mark Ministries*. http://jmm.aaa.net.au/articles/9680.htm. Accessed 7 February 2008.

Culbertson, Philip. ed. *Counselling Issues and South Pacific Communities*. Auckland: Accent Publications, 1997.

DeYoung, Curtis Paul, Michael O. Emerson, George Yancey, and Karen Chai Kim. *United by Faith: The Multiracial Congregation as an Answer to the Problem of Race*. New York: Oxford University Press, 2003.

Dickson, John. *History of the Presbyterian Church of New Zealand*. Dunedin: J. Wilkie & Co., 1899.

Dodd, C. H. *The Epistle to the Romans*. The Moffatt New Testament Commentary. London: Hodder and Stoughton Ltd., 1932.

Don, Alexander. "Our Chinese Mission." *The N.Z. Presbyterian* (October 1, 1884): 64-65.

— "Chinese Mission Work in Otago: Annual Up-country Tour 1894-95." *The Christian Outlook* 071, no. 24 (1895). Hocken Pamphlet Collection, University of Otago.

— "Dunedin Chinese Mission Station." *The Christian Outlook* 2, no. 3 (15 February 1896). Hocken Pamphlet Collection, University of Otago.

— "Chinese Mission Report." *The Christian Outlook* 3, no. 4 (20 February 1896). Hocken Pamphlet Collection, University of Otago.

— "Chinese Mission in Wellington." *The Christian Outlook* 4, no. 15 (8 May 1897). Hocken Pamphlet Collection, University of Otago.

— "Chinese Mission Work in Otago: Annual Up-country Tour 1900-01." *The Christian Outlook* 074, no. 24 (1901). Hocken Pamphlet Collection, University of Otago.

Dougherty, Kevin D. "How Monochromatic is Church Membership? Racial-ethnic Diversity in a Religious Community." *Sociology of Religion* 64, no. 1 (2004): 65-85.

DuBose, Francis M. "The Journal of Matthew Ricci." In *Classics of Christian Missions*, ed. Francis M. DuBose, 167-172. Nashville, TN: Broadman Press, 1979.

Duncan, Betty K. "Christianity: Pacific Island Traditions." In *Religions of New Zealanders*, ed. Peter Donovan, 128-141. Palmerston North: Dunmore Press, 1990.

Duncan, George S. *The Epistle of Paul to the Galatians*. The Moffatt New Testament Commentary. London: Hodder and Stoughton Ltd., 1934.

Dunn, James G. D. *Jesus Remembered: Christianity in the Making*. Vol. 1. Grand Rapids, MI: William B. Eerdmans, 2003.

— *Beginning From Jerusalem: Christianity in the Making*. Vol. 2. Grand Rapids, MI: William B. Eerdmans, 2009.

Eagleton, Terry. *The Idea of Culture*. Oxford: Blackwell, 2000.

Ebaugh, Helen Rose. "Religion and the New Immigrants." In *Handbook of the Sociology of Religion*, ed. M. Dillon, 225-239. Cambridge: Cambridge University Press, 2003.

Edwards, Korie L. "Bring Race to the Center: The Importance of Race in Racially Diverse Religious Organizations." *Journal for the Scientific Study of Religion* 47, no. 1 (2008): 5-9.

Elder, John R. *The History of the Presbyterian Church of New Zealand 1840-1940*. Christchurch: Presbyterian Bookroom, 1940.

Elmer, Duane. *Cross-Cultural Conflict: Building Relationships for Effective Ministry*. Downers Grove, IL: InterVarsity Press, 1993.

Elsmore, Bronwyn. "Baha'i Faith." In *Religions of New Zealanders*, ed. Peter Donovan, 20-31. Palmerston North: Dunmore Press, 1990.

Emerson, Michael O., and Christian Smith. *Divided by Faith: Evangelical Religion and the Problem of Race in America*. New York: Oxford University Press, 2000.

Emerson, Michael O., and B. Christerson. "The Cost of Diversity in Religious Organizations: An In-depth Case Study." *Sociology of Religion* 64, no. 2 (2003): 163-181.

Emerson, Michael O., and C. Karen Kim. "Multiracial Congregations: An Analysis of their Development and a Typology." *Journal for the Scientific Study of Religion* 42, no. 2 (2003): 217-227.

Emerson, Michael O., and Rodney Woo. *People of the Dream: Multiracial Congregations in the United States*. Princeton, NJ: Princeton University Press, 2006.

Emerson, Michael O. "Why a Forum on Racially and Ethnically Diverse Congregations?" *Journal for the Scientific Study of Religion* 47, no. 1 (2008): 1-4.

Ferguson, Everett. *The Church of Christ: A Biblical Ecclesiology for Today*. Grand Rapids, MI: William B. Eerdmans, 1996.

Ferguson, Sinclair B., and David F. Wright, eds. *New Dictionary of Theology*. Leicester: InterVarsity Press, 1988.

Fischer, Michael M. J. "Ethnicity and the Post-Modern Arts of Memory." In *Writing Culture: The Poetics and Politics of Ethnography*, ed. James Clifford and George E Marcus, 194-233. Berkeley, CA: University of California Press, 1986.

Fitzgerald, Thomas K. *Metaphors of Identity: A Culture Communication Dialogue*. Albany, NY: State University of New York, 1993.

Fitzgerald, Thomas K., and Yvonne J. Underhill-Sem. *Paddling a Multicultural Canoe in Bicultural Waters: Ethnic Identity and Aspirations of Second Generation Cook Islanders in New Zealand*. Christchurch: Macmillan Brown Centre for Pacific Studies, University of Canterbury, 1996.

Fletcher, H. J. *Fletcher of Taupo*. Unpublished manuscript, Wanganui, New Zealand, 1975.

Foster, Charles. *Embracing Diversity: Leadership in Multicultural Congregations*. Bethesda, MD: Alban Institute, 1997.

France, R. T. *The Gospel According To Matthew: An Introduction and Commentary*. Leicester: InterVarsity Press, 1985.

Garces-Foley, Kathleen. "Comparing Catholic and Evangelical Integration Efforts." *Journal for the Scientific Study of Religion* 47, no. 1 (2008): 17-22.

Gardenz, Pablo T. *Called from the Jews and from the Gentiles: Pauline Ecclesiology in Romans 9-11*. Wissenschaftliche Untersuchungen zum Neuen Testament 2, Reihe, 267. Tübigen: Mohr Siebeck, 2009.

Giles, Kevin, *What on Earth is the Church? A Biblical and Theological Enquiry*. London: SPCK, 1995.

Gill, William Wyatt. *From Darkness to Light in Polynesia*. London: London Missionary Society, 1894.

Gittins, Anthony J. "The Universal in the Local: Power, Piety and Paradox in the Formation of Missionary Community." In *Mission and Culture: The Louis J. Luzbetak Lectures*, ed. Stephen B. Bevans. The American Society of Missiology Series, 133-87. Maryknoll, NY: Orbis, 2012.

Goroncy, Jason A. *Social Identity, Ethnicity, and the Gospel of Reconciliation*. Unpublished paper. Knox Centre for Ministry and Leadership, Dunedin, New Zealand, 2012.

Grenz, Stanley J. *Theology for the Community of God*. Grand Rapids, MI: William B. Eerdmans; and Vancouver: Regent College Publishing, 2000.

Greenwood, Robin. *Practicing Ministry: The Task of the Local Church*. London: SPCK, 1996.

Gunton, Colin E. *The One, the Three and the Many: God, Creation and the Culture of Modernity*. The Bampton Lectures, 1992. Cambridge: Cambridge University Press, 1993.

Guthrie, Donald. *New Testament Introduction*, 3rd edition (revised). London: InterVarsity Press, 1970.

Hanciles, Jehu J. "Migration and Mission: The Religious Significance of the North-South Divide." In *Mission in the 21st Century: Exploring the Five Marks of Global Mission*, ed. Andrew Walls and Cathy Ross, 118-129. London: Darton, Longman and Todd, 2008.

Hardy, Daniel W. "The Future of Theology in a Complex World." In *Christ and Context: The Confrontation between Gospel and Culture*, ed. Hilary D. Regan and Alan J. Torrance, 21-42. Edinburgh: T&T Clark, 1993.

Harper, Brad, and Paul Louis Metzger. *Exploring Ecclesiology: An Evangelical and Ecumenical Introduction*. Grand Rapids, MI: Brazos Press, 2009.

Hays, Richard B. "The Letter to the Galatians." In *The New Interpreter's Bible*, Vol. XI, ed. Leander E. Keck, 181-348. Nashville, TN: Abingdon Press, 2000.

Hellerman, Joseph H. *Jesus and the People of God: Reconfiguring Ethnic Identity*. Sheffield: Sheffield Phoenix Press, 2007.

Hesselgrave, David J. and Edward Rommen. *Contextualization: Meanings, Methods and Models*. Grand Rapids, MI: Baker Book House, 1989.

Hodge, Damon Hodge. "Separation of Church and Race." *Las Vegas Weekly*, 28 June 2005. http://www.lasvegasweekly.com/coverstory. Accessed 24 May 2006.

Hooper, Anthony. "The Migration of Cook Islanders to New Zealand." *Journal of Polynesian Society* 70, no. 1 (1965): 11-17.

Horrell, David G. *The Social Ethos of the Corinthian Correspondence: Interests and Ideology from 1 Corinthians to 1 Clement*. Studies of the New Testament and its World. Edinburgh: T&T Clark, 1996.

Hooker, Morna D. *The Gospel According to St. Mark*. Black's New Testament Commentaries. London: A & C Black, 1991.

Houtz, L. E. "Instructional Strategy Change and the Attitude and Achievement of Seventh and Eighth-grade Science Students." *Journal of Research in Science Teaching* 32, no. 6 (1995): 629-648.

"In the Presence of All Peoples: Celebrating Cultural Diversity." In *Caritas Social Justice Series*, 10, 5. Wellington: Caritas Aotearoa New Zealand, 2005.

Inbody, Tyron. *The Faith of the Christian Church: An Introduction to Theology*. Grand Rapids, MI: William B. Eerdmans, 2005.

Irvine, Susan. "'Teacher' Don: The Mission to the Chinese in Otago." In *Building God's Own Country: Historical Essays on Religion in New Zealand*, ed. John Stenhouse and Jane Thompson, 155-168. Dunedin: University of Otago Press, 2004.

Irwin, James. *From Dependence to Autonomy*. Annual Lecture in Whakatane. Dunedin: Presbyterian Historical Society, 1984.

Jamieson, Alan. *A Churchless Faith: Faith Journeys beyond Evangelical, Pentecostal and Charismatic Churches*. Wellington: Philip Garside Publishing Ltd, 2002.

Jeremias, Joachim. *Jesus' Promise to the Nations*. Trans. S. H. Hooke. London: SCM Press, 1958.

Jeung, Russell. *Faithful Generations: Race and New Asian American Churches*. New Brunswick, NJ: Rutgers University Press, 2005.

Joseph, Tokerau. "Cracked Coconuts: An Exploration of Why Young Cook Islanders are Leaving Cook Islander Congregations of the Presbyterian Church of Aotearoa New Zealand." M.Th. thesis, University of Otago, 2005.

Kamo, Lalomilo. *The Samoan Culture and the Christian Gospel*. Suva, Fiji: University of the South Pacific, 1996.

Kasper, Walter. "That They May All Be One." In *Christian Doctrine: A Reader*, ed. Lindsay Hall, Murray Rae, and Steve Holmes, 384-85. London: SCM Press, 2010.

Keary, Anne. "Colonial Constructs and Cross-Cultural Interaction: Comparing Missionary/Indigenous Encounters in Northwestern America and Eastern Australia." In *Beyond Conversion and Syncretism: Indigenous Encounters with Missionary Christianity, 1800-2000*, ed. David Lindenfeld and Miles Richardson, 243-298. Oxford: Berghahn Books, 2012.

Kelly, J. N. D. *Early Christian Creeds*, 3rd edition. London: Longman Group Limited, 1972.

Kim, Rebecca Y. "Second-Generation Korean American Evangelicals: Ethnic, Multiethnic, or White Campus Ministries?" *Sociology of Religion* 65, no. 1 (2004): 19-34.

Krause, Neal. "Exploring Race Differences in the Relationship between Social Interaction with Clergy and Feelings of Self-worth in Late Life." *Sociology of Religion* 64, no. 2 (2004): 183-205.

Kselman, John S. "Grace." In *The Anchor Bible Dictionary*, Vol. 2, ed. David Noel Freedman, 1084-1086. New York: Doubleday, 1992.

Kuecker, Aaron. *The Spirit and the "Other": Social Identity, Ethnicity and Intergroup Reconciliation in Luke-Acts*. New York: T&T Clark, 2011.

Küng, Hans. *The Church*. Trans. Ray and Rosaleen Ockenden. New York: Sheed & Ward, 1968.

Kwon, V. H. *Entrepreneurship and Religion: Korean Immigrants in Houston, Texas*. New York: Garland, 1997.

Lampe, Peter. *From Paul to Valentinus: Christians at Rome in the First Two Centuries*. Trans. Michael Steinhauser, ed. Marshall D. Johnson. Minneapolis, MN: Fortress Press, 2003.

Lange, Raeburn. *Island Ministers: Indigenous Leadership in Nineteenth Century Pacific Islands Christianity*. Christchurch: Macmillan Brown Centre for Pacific Studies, University of Canterbury, 2005.

— "Ordained Ministry in Māori Christianity 1853-1900." *Journal of Religious History* 27, no. 1 (February 2003): 47-66.

— *The Origins of the Christian Ministry in the Cook Islands and Samoa*. MacMillan Brown Working Paper Series, no. 6. Christchurch: MacMillan Brown Center for Pacific Studies, University of Canterbury, 1997.

Laughton, John G. *From Forest Trail to City Street: The Story of the Presbyterian Church among the Māori People*. Christchurch: Presbyterian Bookroom, 1961.

Law, Eric H. F. *Sacred Acts, Holy Change: Faithful Diversity and Practical Transformation*. St. Louis, MO: Chalice Press, 2002.

— *The Bush Was Blazing But Not Consumed: Developing a Multicultural Community through Dialogue and Liturgy*. St. Louis, MO: Chalice Press, 1996.

— *The Wolf Shall Dwell with the Lamb: Spirituality for Leadership in a Multicultural Community*. St. Louis, MO: Chalice Press, 1993.

Leith, John H., ed. *Creeds of the Churches: A Reader in Christian Doctrine from the Bible to the Present*. New York: Double Day & Company Inc., 1963.

Lincoln, Andrew T. *Ephesians*. Word Biblical Commentary 42. Dallas, TX: Word Books, 1990.

Lineham, Peter. "It's a New World Out There." In *The Religious Question: Findings from the 1996 Census*, prepared by the Christian Research Association of Aotearoa New Zealand, 61-73. Auckland: The Christian Research Association, 2000.

Longnecker, Richard N. *Galatians*. Word Biblical Commentary 41. Dallas, TX: Word Books, 1990.

Lovett, Richard. *The History of the London Missionary Society, 1795-1895*. Vol. 2. London: Frowd, 1899.

Lutz, Jesse G. "A Profile of Chinese Protestant Evangelists in the Mid-Nineteenth Century." In *Authentic Chinese Christianity: Preludes to its Development (Nineteenth and Twentieth Centuries)*, ed. Ku Wei-ying and Koen De Ridder, 67-86. Leuven: Leuven University Press, 2001.

Lyall, David. *Integrity of Pastoral Care*. London: SPCK, 2001.

Macquarrie, John. *Theology, Church and Ministry*. London: SCM Press, 1986.

Manson, T. W. *The Sayings of Jesus*. London: SCM Press, 1949.

Māori Synod, Presbyterian Church of New Zealand. *A Māori View of the Hunn Report*. Christchurch: Presbyterian Bookroom, 1961.

Maretu. *Cannibals and Converts: Radical Change in the Cook Islands*. Trans. and ed. Marjorie T. Crocombe. Suva, Fiji: Institute of Pacific Studies, University of the South Pacific, 1983.

Marti, Gerardo Marti. *A Mosaic of Believers: Diversity and Innovation in a Multiethnic Church*. Bloomington, IN: Indiana University Press, 2005.

— "Fluid Ethnicity and Ethnic Transcendence in Multiracial Church." *Journal for the Scientific Study of Religion* 47, no. 1 (2008): 11-16.

Matheson, Peter. "The Settler Church 1840-1870." In *Presbyterians in Aotearoa 1840-1990*, ed. Dennis McEldowney, 15-42. Wellington: Presbyterian Church of New Zealand, 1990.

— *First Church of Otago: The People's Church*. Dunedin: First Church of Otago, 1998.

McClintock, Wayne. "Sociological Critique of the Homogeneous Unit Principle." *Review of Religion* 77, no. 305 (January 1988): 107-116.

McGavran, Donald A. *Church Growth: Strategies that Work*. Nashville, TN: Abingdon Press, 1980.

— *The Bridges of God: A Study in the Strategy of Missions*. London: World Dominion Press, 1957.

— *The Clash between Christianity and Culture*. Washington, DC: Canon Press, 1974.

McGrath, Alister E. *Christian Theology: An Introduction*. Oxford: Blackwell, 1994.

McKean, John. *The Church in a Special Colony: A History of the Presbyterian Synod of Otago and Southland 1866-1991*. Dunedin: Synod of Otago and Southland, 1994.

Meeks, Wayne A. and Robert L. Wilken. *Jews and Christians in Antioch: In the First Four Centuries of the Common Era*. Society of Biblical Literature, Sources for Biblical Study 13. Missoula, MT: Scholars Press, 1978.

Meier, John P. "Antioch." In *Antioch and Rome: New Testament Cradles of Catholic Christianity*, ed. Raymond E. Brown and John P. Meier, 11-86. New York: Paulist Press, 1983.

Migliore, Daniel L. *Faith Seeking Understanding: An Introduction to Christian Theology*. Grand Rapids, MI: William B. Eerdmans, 1991.

Moffatt, James. *The First Epistle of Paul to the Corinthians*. The Moffatt New Testament Commentary. London: Hodder and Stoughton Ltd., 1938.

Moltmann, Jürgen. *The Church in the Power of the Spirit: A Contribution to Messianic Ecclesiology*. Trans. Margaret Kohl. Minneapolis, MN: Fortress Press, 1993.

— *The Open Church: Invitation to a Messianic Lifestyle*. London: SCM Press, 1978.

Multi-Crosscultural Congregations: A Kitset for God's People on the Way. Auckland: Christian Research Association of Aotearoa New Zealand, 1999.

Nachowtz, Todd. "New Zealand as a Multireligious Society: Recent Census Figures and Some Relevant Implications." *Aotearoa Ethnic Network Journal* 2, no. 2 (August 2007): 1-8.

Newbigin, Lesslie. *The Gospel in a Pluralistic Society*. Grand Rapids, MI: William B. Eerdmans, 1989.

Ng, James. *The Presbyterian Church of New Zealand and the Chinese*. Christchurch: Presbyterian Historical Society, 1987.

Nokise, Uili Feleterika. "A History of the Pacific Islanders' Congregational Church in New Zealand 1943-1969." M.Th. thesis, University of Otago, 1978.

O'Day, Gail R. "The Gospel of John." In *The New Interpreter's Bible*, Vol. IX, ed. Leander E. Keck, 491-865. Nashville, TN: Abingdon Press, 1995.

Omi, M., and H. Winant. *Racial Formation in the United States: From 1960s to 1990s.* New York: Routledge, 1994.

Padilla, C. René. "The Unity of the Church and the Homogeneous Unit Principle." *International Bulletin of Missionary Research* 6, no. 1 (January 1982): 23-30.

Paik, Lak-Geoon George. *The History of Protestant Missions in Korea 1832-1910*, 3rd edition. Seoul: Yonsei University Press, 1980.

Pannenberg, Wolfhart. *The Apostles' Creed: In Light of Today's Questions.* Trans. Margaret Kohl. London: SCM Press, 1972.

Paterson, Lachy. "The Rise and Fall of Women Field Workers within the Presbyterian Māori Mission, 1907-1970." In *Mana Māori and Christianity*, ed. Hugh Morrison, Lachy Peterson, Brett Knowles, and Murray Rae, 179-204. Wellington: Huia Publishers, 2012.

Perkins, Pheme. "The Letter to the Ephesians." In *The New Interpreter's Bible*, Vol. XI, ed. Leander E. Keck, 349-466. Nashville, TN: Abingdon Press, 2002.

Prentiss, Craig R. ed. *Religion and the Creation of Race and Ethnicity: An Introduction.* New York: New York University Press, 2003.

Rae, Murray. "The Subversive Theology of Rua Kēnana." In *Mana Māori and Christianity*, ed. Hugh Morrison, Lachy Peterson, Brett Knowles, and Murray Rae, 223-242. Wellington: Huia Publishers, 2012.

Rakena, Rua D. *The Māori Response to the Gospel: A Study of Māori-Pakeha Relations in the Māori Methodist Missions from its Beginnings to the Present Day.* Auckland: Wesley Historical Society, 1971.

Riini, Sonny, and Diane Gilliam-Knight. "An Historical Perspective Helps." In *He Taonga hei Whakatu Honohono: A Gift Towards Partnership.* Te Hinota Māori, Book 1, 12-15. Wellington: Presbyterian Church of Aotearoa New Zealand, 1992.

Ross, J. "The Christian Dawn in Korea." *The Missionary Review of the World* 3, no. 4 (1890): 242-243.

Sampley, J. Paul. "The First Letter to the Corinthians." In *The New Interpreter's Bible*, Vol. X, ed. Leander E. Keck, 771-1003. Nashville, TN: Abingdon Press, 2002.

Sanday, W., and A. C. Headlam. *The Epistle to the Romans*, 5th edition. International Critical Commentary. Edinburgh: T. & T. Clark, 1902.

Shogren, Gary S. "Grace." In *The Anchor Bible Dictionary*, Vol. 2, ed. David Noel Freedman, 1086-1088. New York: Doubleday, 1992.

Sim, David C. *The Gospel of Matthew and Christian Judaism: The History and Social Setting of the Matthean Community*. Edinburgh: T. & T. Clark, 1998.

Singer, Angela. "Welcome Home: Church Considers Cultural Change for Asian Members." *SPANZ* 54 (Winter 2013): 4-5.

Singh, Pritam. "Sikhism." In *Religions of New Zealanders*, ed. Peter Donovan, 221-237. Palmerston North: Dunmore Press, 1990.

Sinha, Jill W., Amy Hillier, Ram A. Cnaan, and Charlene C. McGrew. "Proximity Matters: Exploring Relationships among Neighborhoods, Congregations, and the Residential Patterns of Members." *Journal for the Scientific Study of Religion* 46, no. 2 (2007): 245-260.

Smith, Abraham. "The First Letter to the Thessalonians." In *The New Interpreter's Bible*, Vol. XI, ed. Leander E. Keck, 671-686. Nashville, TN: Abingdon Press, 2002.

Smith, J. N. *Upon them the Light Shined: A Brief History of the Presbyterian Māori Mission*. Auckland: Presbyterian Church of New Zealand, 1952.

Southern, Richard, and Robert Norton. *Cracking Your Congregation's Code: Mapping Your Spiritual DNA to Create Your Future*. San Francisco: Jossey-Bass, 2001.

Standaert, Nicolas, ed. *Handbook of Christianity in China, 635-1800*. Vol. 1. Leiden: Brill, 2001a.

Stephen Spence. *Parting of the Ways: The Roman Church as a Case Study*. Interdisciplinary Studies in Ancient Culture and Religion 5. Leuven: Peeters, 2004.

Stevens, David. E. *God's New Humanity: A Biblical Theology of Multiethnicity for the Church*. Eugene, OR: Wipf & Stock, 2012.

Stone, John. *Race and Ethnicity: Comparative and Theoretical Approaches*. Oxford: Blackwell, 2003.

Tekaawa, Wayne. *Ko te Amorangi ki mua, ko te hapai o ki muri*. Inaugural Lecture, Knox Centre for Ministry and Leadership, Dunedin, 2013.

The Book of Order of the Presbyterian Church of Aotearoa New Zealand. Wellington: Presbyterian Church of Aotearoa New Zealand, 2008.

"The Chinese in Otago." *The Evangelist* 4, no. 5 (1 May 1872): 129-132.

"The Missionary to the Chinese in Otago." *The Evangelist* 3, no. 4 (1 April 1871): 124.

The Religious Question: Findings from the 1996 Census, prepared by the Christian Research Association of Aotearoa New Zealand. Auckland: The Christian Research Association, 2000.

Tiatia, Jemaima. *Caught between Cultures: A New Zealand-born Pacific Island Perspective*. Auckland: Christian Research Association, 1998.

Titus, Paul. "Multicultural NZ and the Changing Face of Today's Church." *Touchstone* 1. Christchurch: The Methodist Church of New Zealand, September, 2009.

Torrance, T. F. *Royal Priesthood: A Theology of Ordained Ministry*, 2nd edition. Edinburgh: T&T Clark, 1993.

Tseng, Timothy. "Asian American Religious Leadership Today: A Preliminary Inquiry." In *Pulpit and Pew: Research on Pastoral Leadership*, 1-52. Durham, NC: Duke University Divinity School, 2005.

Tucker, H. W. *Memoir of the Life and Episcopate of George Augustus Selwyn*. Vol. 2. London: Gardner, 1879.

Underwood, H. G. *The Call of Korea*. New York: Leming H. Revell Company, 1908.

Viradhammo, Ajahn. "Buddhism." In *Religions of New Zealanders*, ed. Peter Donovan, 32-45. Palmerston North: Dunmore Press, 1990.

Vogel, Stuart. *Asian-Ethnic Congregations and the PCANZ*. Discussion Paper 3 (unpublished paper), presented at the General Assembly of the PCANZ, 2012.

— *Inklings of an Altered State: Counter-imaging the Presbyterian Church of Aotearoa New Zealand within a Culturally Diverse Society*. Discussion Paper 1 (unpublished paper), presented at the General Assembly of the PCANZ, 2012.

— "Principles and Guidelines for Parishes and Presbyteries." A Handbook prepared by the committee of the Development of Asian Ministries within the Presbyterian Church of Aotearoa New Zealand. Unpublished, 1995.

— *The Self-understanding of a Multi-Ethnic Church*. Discussion Paper 2 (unpublished paper), presented at the General Assembly of the PCANZ, 2012.

Volf, Miroslav. *After our Likeness: The Church as the Image of the Trinity*. Grand Rapids, MI: William B. Eerdmans, 1998.

Wagner, C. Peter. "How Ethical is the Homogeneous Unit Principle?" *Occasional Bulletin of Missionary Research* 2, no. 1 (January 1978): 12-19.

— *Our Kind of People: The Ethical Dimensions of Church Growth in America*. Atlanta, GA: John Knox Press, 1979.

Walls, Andrew F. *The Missionary Movement in Christian History: Studies in the Transmission of Faith*. Maryknoll, NY: Orbis Books, 1996.

Walters, J. C. "Romans, Jews and Christians: The Impact of the Romans on Jewish-Christian Relations". In *Judaism and Christianity in First Century Rome*, ed. Karl P. Donfried and Peter Richardson, 175-195. Grand Rapids, MI: William B. Eerdmans, 1998.

Ward, Alan. *A Show of Justice: Racial "Amalgamation" in Nineteenth Century New Zealand*. Auckland: Auckland University Press, 1995.

Ward, Graham. *Cultural Transformation and Religious Practice*. Cambridge: Cambridge University Press, 2005.

Ward, Kevin. "Christendom, Clericalism, Church and Context." *Stimulus* 10, no. 1 (February 2002): 61-69.

— *Cultural Diversity and Unity in Christ: The Presbyterian Church of Aotearoa New Zealand in a Land of Many Cultures*. Unpublished paper. Dunedin: Knox Centre for Ministry and Leadership, 2013.

— "It might be Emerging, but is it Church?" *Stimulus* 17, no. 4 (November 2009): 2-13.

Warner, R. S. "The Korean Immigrant Church as a Case Model." In *Korean Americans and their Religions: Pilgrims and Missionaries from a Different Shore*, ed. H. Y. Kwon, K. C. Kim, and R. S. Warner, 25-52. University Park, PA: Pennsylvania State University, 2001.

Williams, C. Peter. *The Ideal of the Self-Governing Church*. Leiden: Brill, 1990.

Williams, John. *A Narrative of Missionary Enterprises in the South Sea Islands*. London: John Snow, 1842.

Willimon, William H. *Pastor: The Theology and Practice of Ordained Ministry*. Nashville, TN: Abingdon Press, 2002.

Witek, John W. "Christianity and China: Universal Teaching from the West." In *China and Christianity: Burdened Past, Hopeful Future*, ed. Stephen Uhalley Jr. and Xiaoxin Wu, 11-28. New York: M. E. Sharpe, 2000.

Witherington, Ben. *Conflict and Community in Corinth: A Socio-Rhetorical Commentary on 1 and 2 Corinthians*. Grand Rapids, MI: William B. Eerdmans, 1995.

World Council of Churches, *Christian Perspectives on Theological Anthropology: A Faith and Order Study Document.* Faith and Order Paper 199. Geneva: World Council of Churches, 2005.

Wright, N. T. "The Letter to the Romans." In *The New Interpreter's Bible*, Vol. X, ed. Leander E. Keck, 393-770. Nashville, TN: Abingdon Press, 2002.

Zizioulas, John D. *Being as Communion: Studies in Personhood and the Church.* London: Darton, Longman and Todd, 1985.

Church Reports and Correspondence

Annual Report, Chinese Presbyterian Church of Dunedin, 1905.

Annual Report, Chinese Presbyterian Church of Dunedin, 1907.

Annual Report, Chinese Presbyterian Church of Dunedin, 1909.

Annual Report, Chinese Presbyterian Church of Dunedin, 1960.

Correspondence, Keith W. Robertson of the Dunedin Chinese Presbyterian Church to Rev. Jusak Susabda, Convenor of the Advisory Committee on Asian Ministries, 9 October 1997.

Correspondence, Stuart Vogel (Secretary Asian Advisory Council) to Tokerau Joseph, 12 June 2012.

Council of Asian Congregations Report. Assembly Reports, F16-1. General Assembly, Presbyterian Church of Aotearoa New Zealand, 2004.

"General and Financial Statistics 1944, Dunedin Presbytery." In *Proceedings of General Assembly 1944*, Presbyterian Church of New Zealand. Dunedin, PCANZ Archives.

"General and Financial Statistics 1948, Dunedin Presbytery." In *Proceedings of General Assembly 1948*, Presbyterian Church of New Zealand, 350-351. Dunedin: PCANZ Archives.

"General and Financial Statistics 1954, Dunedin Presbytery." In *Proceedings of General Assembly 1954*, Presbyterian Church of New Zealand, 256a. Dunedin: PCANZ Archives.

Miller, A. L. "Minister's Report." Chinese Church of Dunedin Annual Report, 1940. Dunedin: PCANZ Archives.

— "Report on the Work among the Chinese of the South Island." In *Proceedings of General Assembly 1942*, 87-88, Presbyterian Church of New Zealand, 1942. Dunedin: PCANZ Archives.

— "Chinese Church, Dunedin Report." June 30th 1943. Dunedin: PCANZ Archives.

McNeur, George. *Mission to the Chinese in New Zealand*. Report on the Work among the Chinese in the South Island, July 20, 1944-June 30, 1945. Dunedin: PCANZ Archives.

Minutes, Session 8.14. General Assembly, Presbyterian Church of Aotearoa New Zealand, 1993.

Proceedings of the General Assembly 1969, 160-61. Wellington: Presbyterian Church of New Zealand, 1969.

Vogel, Stuart. Council of Asian Congregations Report. Auckland, 2005.

Endnotes

1 Alister E. McGrath, *Christian Theology: An Introduction* (Oxford: Blackwell Publishers Inc., 1994), 405.

2 Ibid.

3 John Stone, *Race and Ethnicity: Comparative and Theoretical Approaches* (Oxford: Blackwell, 2003), 33.

4 Michael M. J. Fischer, "Ethnicity and the Post-Modern Arts of Memory," in *Writing Culture: The Poetics and Politics of Ethnography*, ed. James Clifford and George E Marcus, 194-233 (Berkeley, CA: University of California Press, 1986), 195.

5 Michael O. Emerson, "Why a Forum on Racially and Ethnically Diverse Congregations?," *JSSR* 47, no. 1 (2008): 1-4, 2. Emerson states that in the 1960s, only about 12% of Americans were people of colour, mostly African Americans. As of 2008, it is estimated that that percentage has tripled to about 35%. See also M. Omi and H. Winant, *Racial Formation in the United States: From 1960s to 1990s* (New York: Routledge, 1994).

6 Michael O. Emerson and C. Karen Kim, "Multiracial Congregations: An Analysis of their Development and a Typology," *JSSR* 42, no. 2 (2003): 217-227, 217. See also Mark Chaves, *National Congregations Study* (Tucson, AZ: Department of Sociology, University of Arizona, 1999).

7 Ibid.

8 Ibid.

9 Kevin D. Dougherty, "How Monochromatic is Church Membership? Racial-ethnic Diversity in Religious Community," *SR* 64, no. 1 (2004): 65-85, 68.

10 Ibid., 79-80. Dougherty notes that income diversity in a congregation does not significantly relate to ethnic diversity and that the more diverse a congregation or parish is in terms of education, the more diverse it is racially.

11 Jill Witmer Sinha, Amy Hillier, Ram A. Cnaan and Charlene C. McGrew, "Proximity Matters: Exploring Relationships among Neighborhoods, Congregations, and the Residential Patterns of Members," *JSSR* 46, no. 2 (2007): 245-260, 258.

12 Ibid.

13 Emerson and Kim, "Multiracial Congregations," 219. They argue that religious congregations reflect the racial composition of the neighbourhoods and environments in which they are located. If neighbourhoods are largely made up of a particular ethnic group, then the church in that area would mostly likely reflect that as well.

Endnotes

14 George A. Yancey, *One Body One Spirit: Principles of Successful Multiracial Churches* (Downers Grove, IL: InterVarsity Press, 2003), 27.

15 Michael O. Emerson and Christian Smith, *Divided by Faith: Evangelical Religion and the Problem of Race in America* (New York: Oxford University Press, 2000), 137.

16 Ibid., 145.

17 Emerson and Kim, "Multiracial Congregations," 219.

18 C. Peter Wagner, "How Ethical is the Homogeneous Unit Principle?," *Occasional Bulletin of Missionary Research* 2, no. 1 January (1978): 12-19, 13.

19 C. Peter Wagner, *Our Kind of People: The Ethical Dimensions of Church Growth in America* (Atlanta, GA: John Knox Press, 1979).

20 Donald McGavran, *Church Growth: Strategies that Work* (Nashville, TN: Abingdon Press, 1980), 227. See also Donald McGavran, *The Clash between Christianity and Culture* (Washington, DC: Canon Press, 1974), 23.

21 C. René Padilla, "The Unity of the Church and the Homogeneous Unit Principle," *International Bulletin of Missionary Research* 6, no. 1 (January 1982): 23-30, 29. See also Wayne McClintock, "Sociological Critique of the Homogeneous Unit Principle," *Review of Religion* 77, no. 305 (January 1988): 107-116.

22 Yancey, *One Body One Spirit*, 35. Yancey found that 66.1% of multiracial churches have grown versus 57.1% of mono-racial churches.

23 Michael O. Emerson and B. Christerson, "The Cost of Diversity in Religious Organizations: An In-depth Case Study," *SR* 64, no. 2 (2003): 163-181; B. Christerson, B. K. L. Edwards and M. O. Emerson, *Against All Odds: The Struggle for Racial Integration in Religious Organizations* (New York: New York University Press, 2005); M. O. Emerson, with Rodney Woo, *People of the Dream: Multiracial Congregations in the United States* (Princeton, NJ: Princeton University Press, 2006).

24 Emerson and Christerson, "The Cost of Diversity," 166.

25 Nancy T. Ammerman, *Congregations and Community* (New Brunswick, NJ: Rutgers University Press, 1997).

26 Nancy T. Ammerman, Jackson W. Carroll, Carl S. Dudley and William McKinney, eds., *Studying Congregations: A New Handbook* (Nashville, TN: Abingdon Press, 1998).

27 Charles Foster, *Embracing Diversity: Leadership in Multicultural Congregations* (Bethesda, MD: Alban Institute, 1997).

28 Ibid., 116-122.

29 Gerardo Marti, *A Mosaic of Believers: Diversity and Innovation in a Multiethnic Church* (Bloomington, IN: Indiana University Press, 2005).

30 Ibid., 156.

31 Damon Hodge, "Separation of Church and Race," *Las Vegas Weekly*, 28 June 2005, //http.www.lasvegasweekly.com/coverstory, accessed 24 May 2006.

32 Emerson and Kim, "Multiracial Congregations," 224.

33 Neal Krause, "Exploring Race Differences in the Relationship between Social Interaction with Clergy and Feelings of Self-worth in Late Life," *SR* 64, no. 2 (2004): 183-205.

34 Ibid.

35 Helen Rose Ebaugh, "Religion and the New Immigrants," in *Handbook of the Sociology of Religion*, ed. M. Dillon, 225-239 (Cambridge: Cambridge University Press, 2003), 232-33. See also R. S. Warner, "The Korean Immigrant Church as a Case Model," in *Korean Americans and their Religions: Pilgrims and Missionaries from a Different Shore*, ed. H. Y. Kwon, K. C. Kim and R. S. Warner, 25-52 (University Park, PA: Pennsylvania State University, 2001), 31; and V. H. Kwon, *Entrepreneurship and Religion: Korean Immigrants in Houston, Texas* (New York: Garland, 1997).

36 Ibid.

37 Timothy Tseng, "Asian American Religious Leadership Today: A Preliminary Inquiry," in *Pulpit and Pew: Research on Pastoral Leadership* (Durham, NC: Duke University Divinity School, 2005), 1-52.

38 Ibid, 21-22.

39 Ibid., 21.

40 For research within a Korean context, see Karen Chai, "Competing for the Second Generation: English-language Ministry in a Korean Protestant Church," in *Gatherings in Diaspora: Religious Communities and the New Immigration*, ed. R. Stephen Warner and Judith G. Wittner, 295-331 (Philadelphia: Temple University Press, 1998); and A. Alumkal, "Being Korean, Being Christian: Particularism and Universalism in a Second-generation Congregation," in *Korean Americans and the Religions: Pilgrims and Missionaries from a Different Shore*, ed. H. Y. Kwon, K. C. Kim, and R. S. Warner, 181-192 (University Park, PA: Pennsylvania State University, 2001). For research within a Pacific Islanders' context, see Jemaima Tiatia, *Caught Between Cultures: A New Zealand-born Pacific Island Perspective* (Auckland: Christian Research Association, 1998); Thomas K. Fitzgerald, *Metaphors of Identity: A Culture Communication Dialogue* (Albany, NY: SUNY, 1993), 95; Thomas K. Fitzgerald and Yvonne J. Underhill-Sem, *Paddling a Multicultural Canoe in Bicultural Waters: Ethnic Identity and Aspirations of Second Generation Cook Islanders in New Zealand* (Christchurch: Macmillan Brown Centre for Pacific Studies, University of Canterbury, 1996), 2; Tokerau Joseph, "Cracked Coconuts: An Exploration of Why Young Cook Islanders are leaving Cook Islander Congregations of the Presbyterian Church of Aotearoa New Zealand," M.Th. thesis, University of Otago, 2005.

41 Rebecca Y. Kim, "Second-Generation Korean American Evangelicals: Ethnic, Multiethnic, or White Campus Ministries?" *SR* 65, no. 1 (2004): 19-34.

42 Ibid., 20.

43 Russell Jeung, *Faithful Generations: Race and New Asian American Churches* (New Brunswick, NJ: Rutgers University Press, 2005).

44 Ibid., 150.

45 Ibid., 155.

46 Yancey, *One Body One Spirit*, 87.

47 Ibid., 73.

48 For example, see Alan Jamieson, *A Churchless Faith: Faith Journeys beyond Evangelical, Pentecostal and Charismatic churches* (Wellington: Philip Garside Publishing Ltd, 2002); Kevin Ward, "Christendom, Clericalism, Church and Context," in *Stimulus* 10, no. 1 (February 2002): 61-69; Jemaima Tiatia, *Caught between Cultures: A New Zealand-born Pacific Island Perspective* (Auckland: Christian Research Association, 1998); and Tokerau Joseph, "Cracked Coconuts: An Exploration of Why Young Cook Islanders are Leaving Cook Islander Congregations of the Presbyterian Church of Aotearoa New Zealand," M.Th. thesis, University of Otago, 2005.

49 http://esa.un.org/Migflows/MigrationFlows.aspx, accessed 9 May 2013.

50 "Ethnic groups in New Zealand," http://www.stats.govt.nz/ Census/2006CensusHomePage/QuickStats /quickstats-about-a-subject/ quickstats-about-culture-and-identity, accessed 9 May 2013.

51 "National Ethnic Population Projections: 2006 (base)-2026 Update," http:// www.stats.govt.nz /browse_for_stats/population/estimates_and_projections/ NationalEthnicPopulationProjections_HOTP200626.aspx, accessed 8 October 2012.

52 *The Religious Question: Findings from the 1996 Census*, prepared by the Christian Research Association of Aotearoa New Zealand (Auckland: The Christian Research Association, 2000), 21.

53 Ibid., 21. By prioritising ethnicity level classification, "European only" = single and combinations of European ethnic groups; "Māori" = people who indicated NZ Māori as one of the ethnic groups; "Pacific Islander" = people who indicated a Pacific Islands group as one of the ethnic groups but excludes NZ Māori; "Asian" = people who indicate an Asian group as one of their ethnic groups but excludes NZ Māori and Pacific Islanders; "Other" = ethnic groups not included above.

54 Ibid., 22.

55 Pritam Singh, "Sikhism," in *Religions of New Zealanders*, ed. Peter Donovan, 221-237 (Palmerston North: Dunmore Press, 1990), 235, notes that Sikhism came to New Zealand in 1890. For Buddhism, see Ajahn Viradhammo, "Buddhism," in *Religions of New Zealanders*, ed. Peter Donovan, 32-45

(Palmerston North: Dunmore Press, 1990), who states that although Buddhism was introduced to New Zealand through Chinese gold miners in Otago and Southland since the 1850s, recent growth between 1981 and 1986 can be attributed to immigration from various parts of Asia.

56 Todd Nachowitz, "New Zealand as a Multireligious Society: Recent Census Figures and Some Relevant Implications," *Aotearoa Ethnic Network Journal* 2, no. 2 (August 2007): 1-8, 6.

57 Andrew Butcher and George Wieland, "Go from Your Country: Missiological Reflections on Asian Christians in New Zealand," *Stimulus* 18, no. 1 (February 2010): 2-8, 4.

58 Ibid.

59 *The Religious Question*, 22. Jehovah's Witness had 56% Europeans, 31% Māori, 9% Pacific Islanders, and 2% Asians. Assemblies of God had 48% Europeans, 10% Māori, 36% Pacific Islanders, and 5% Asians. Seventh Day Adventist had 38% Europeans, 12% Māori, 46% Pacific Islanders, and 2% Asians. Mormons had 14% Europeans, 56% Māori, 28% Pacific Islanders, and 1% Asians.

60 Peter Lineham, "It's a New World Out There," in *The Religious Question*, 61-73, 67.

61 Bronwyn Elsmore, "Baha'i Faith," in *Religions of New Zealanders*, ed. Peter Donovan, 20-31 (Palmerston North: Dunmore Press, 1990), 22.

62 Ibid.

63 See Religious Affiliation by Ethnic Group, 2006 Census, http://wdmzpub01. stats.govt.nz/wds /TableViewer.tableView.aspx, accessed 13 May 2013.

64 In the 1996 census Anglican and Presbyterian European numbers were 536,999 and 389,545 respectively. In 2006, they were 443,145 and 291,726 respectively. It is important to note that not all percentages add up to 100 since not all who indicated a religious affiliation indicated an ethnic identity.

65 "In the Presence of All Peoples: Celebrating Cultural Diversity," in *Caritas Social Justice Series*, no. 10, For Social Justice Week 11 to 17 September 2005 (Wellington: Caritas Aotearoa New Zealand, 2005), 5.

66 Ibid. This is reflected in the ethnic representation of census data between 1996 and 2006.

67 See Constitution of the Anglican Church in Aotearoa New Zealand and Polynesia, Part D for Te Pihopatanga o Aotearoa, Part E for Dioceses in New Zealand, and Part F for Diocese of Polynesia, ix (a)-xiv (a).

68 See http://www.anglican.org.nz/About/History.

69 See Law Book of the Methodist Church of New Zealand, section 4.

70 Ibid., Section 4, 15.1-4.

71 Ibid., Section 4, 14.1.1

72 *Multi-Crosscultural Congregations: A Kitset for God's People on the Way* (Auckland: Christian Research Association Aotearoa New Zealand, 1999).

73 Ibid., see Case Study 2 on St. Andrew's Presbyterian Church, Henderson.

74 Ibid., see Case Study 3. Some Māori members of Holy Cross would attend services conducted in Māori at Te Unga Waka Marae

75 J. Paul Sampley, "The First Letter to the Corinthians," in *NIB*, Vol. X, ed. Leander E. Keck, 771-1003 (Nashville, TN: Abingdon Press, 2002), 777. See also Ben Witherington III, *Conflict and Community in Corinth: A Socio-Rhetorical Commentary on 1 and 2 Corinthians* (Grand Rapids, MI: William B. Eerdmans, 1995), 24-29, who suggests that the diversity of socio-economic levels and religious and ethnic backgrounds among Corinthian Christians was undoubtedly an underlying cause of several of the issues that Paul addresses in the epistles. See also David G. Horrell, *The Social Ethos of the Corinthian Correspondence: Interests and Ideology from 1 Corinthians to 1 Clement*, Studies of the New Testament and its World (Edinburgh: T&T Clark, 1996), 91-101.

76 "For it has been reported to me by Chloe's people that there are quarrels among you, my brothers and sisters. What I mean is that each of you says, 'I belong to Paul,' or 'I belong to Apollos,' or 'I belong to Cephas,' or 'I belong to Christ.' Has Christ been divided?" (1 Cor. 1:11-13).

77 Kevin Giles, *What on Earth is the Church? A Biblical and Theological Enquiry* (London: SPCK, 1995), 103. See also James Moffatt, *The First Epistle of Paul to the Corinthians* (MNTC) (London: Hodder and Stoughton Ltd., 1938), 186, who argues that the corporate organism with many members "acts for the common good of vital health and energy."

78 Everett Ferguson, *The Church of Christ: A Biblical Ecclesiology For Today* (Grand Rapids, MI: William B. Eerdmans, 1996), 401.

79 Richard B. Hays, "The Letter to the Galatians," in *NIB*, Vol. XI, ed. Leander E. Keck, 181-348 (Nashville, TN: Abingdon Press, 2000), 272.

80 Ibid. See also Richard N. Longnecker, *Galatians* (WBC 41) (Dallas, TX: Word Books, 1990), 152, who states that people's relationship together in Christ creates a "new universality of oneness and a new relationship of being God's children."

81 John D. Zizioulas, *Being as Communion: Studies in Personhood and the Church* (London: Darton, Longman and Todd, 1985), 151.

82 John M. G. Barclay, "Universalism and Particularism: Twin Components of Both Judaism and Early Christianity," in *A Vision For The Church: Studies in Early Christian Ecclesiology in Honour of J. P. M. Sweet*, ed. Markus Bockmuehl and Michael B. Thompson, 207-224 (Edinburgh: T&T Clark, 1997), 215.

83 Giles, *What on Earth*, 109. See also George S. Duncan, *The Epistle of Paul to the Galatians* (MNTC) (London: Hodder and Stoughton Ltd., 1934), 123.

84 Jürgen Moltmann, *The Church in the Power of the Spirit: A Contribution to Messianic Ecclesiology*, trans. Margaret Kohl (Minneapolis, MN: Fortress Press, 1993), 189.

85 Ibid., 188.

86 Ibid.

87 Ibid.

88 N. T. Wright, "The Letter to the Romans," in *NIB*, Vol. X, ed. Leander E. Keck, 393-770 (Nashville, TN: Abingdon Press, 2002), 406. Wright suggests that Christian Gentiles and Christian Jews found themselves in "uneasy coexistence." See also Stephen Spence, *Parting of the Ways: The Roman Church as a Case Study* (Interdisciplinary Studies in Ancient Culture and Religion 5) (Leuven: Peeters, 2004), 241, who states that Jewish and Gentile Christians experienced tensions of a sociological nature, not purely of a theological nature; Rudolf Brändle and Ekkehard W. Stegemann, "The Formation of the First 'Christian Congregations' in Rome in the Context of the Jewish Congregations," in *Judaism and Christianity in First-Century Rome*, ed. Karl P. Donfried and Peter Richardson (Grand Rapids, MI: William B. Eerdmans, 1998), 117-127, 123; James D. G. Dunn, *Beginning From Jerusalem*, Christianity in the Making, Vol. 2 (Grand Rapids, MI: William B. Eerdmans, 2009), 1068; William S. Campbell, "The Addressees of Paul's Letter to the Romans: Assemblies of God in House Churches and Synagogues, in *Between Gospel and Election*, ed. Florian Wilk and J. Ross Wagner, with assistance of Frank Schleritt (WUNT 257) (Tübingen: Morh Siebeck, 2010), 171-196, 173; J. C. Walters, "Romans, Jews and Christians: The Impact of the Romans on Jewish-Christian Relations," in *Judaism and Christianity in First Century Rome*, ed. Karl P. Donfried and Peter Richardson (Grand Rapids, MI: William B. Eerdmans, 1998), 175-195, 176; Peter Lampe, *From Paul to Valentinus: Christians at Rome in the First Two Centuries*, trans. Michael Steinhauser, ed. Marshall D. Johnson (Minneapolis, MN: Fortress Press, 2003), 12; W. Sanday and A. C. Headlam, *The Epistle to the Romans*, 5th ed. (ICC) (Edinburgh: T. & T. Clark, 1902), 1895.

89 Jürgen Moltmann, *The Open Church: Invitation to a Messianic Lifestyle* (London: SCM Press, 1978), 27.

90 Ibid.

91 Pheme Perkins, "The Letter to the Ephesians," in *NIB*, Vol. XI, ed. Leander E. Keck, 349-466 (Nashville, TN: Abingdon Press, 2002), 358. See also C. H. Dodd, *The Epistle to the Romans* (MNTC) (London: Hodder and Stoughton Ltd., 1932), 222-224, who posits that the welcoming of Christians, both Jewish and Gentile, in Rome becomes the controlling theme of the Epistle to the Ephesians.

92 Ibid., 362. Perkins proposes that the community envisaged by the letter consists solely of Gentiles being encouraged to remember themselves as brought into a common inheritance with Jewish believers.

Endnotes

93 Andrew T. Lincoln, *Ephesians* (WBC 42) (Dallas, TX: Word Books, 1990), 225; see also Ernest Best, *Ephesians* (ICC) (Edinburgh: T&T Clark, 1998), 36-61.

94 Morna D. Hooker, *The Gospel According to St. Mark* (Black's New Testament Commentaries) (London: A & C Black, 1991), 8, posits a date for Mark between 60-75 C.E., which most scholars support. See also Donald Guthrie, *New Testament Introduction*, 3rd ed. (revised) (London: InterVarsity Press, 1970), 566, who suggests that 1 Thessalonians is the oldest of the Pauline epistles, dated around 51 C.E; and Abraham Smith, "The First Letter to the Thessalonians," in *NIB*, Vol. XI, ed. Leander E. Keck, 671-686 (Nashville, TN: Abingdon Press, 2002), 682.

95 Guthrie, *Introduction*, 23-24. See also T. W. Manson, *The Sayings of Jesus* (London: SCM Press, 1949), 210-11.

96 R. T. France, *The Gospel According to Matthew: An Introduction and Commentary* (Leicester: InterVarsity Press, 1985), 276; see also Manson, *The Sayings*, 210.

97 Raymond E. Brown, *The Gospel According to John (xiii-xxi)* (AB) (New York: Doubleday and Company, 1970), 776.

98 Gail R. O'Day, "The Gospel of John," in *NIB*, Vol. IX, ed. Leander E. Keck, 491-865 (Nashville, TN: Abingdon Press, 1995), 794-95. See also Mark Edwards, *John* (Oxford: Blackwell, 2004), 161; Frederick Dale Bruner, *The Gospel of John: A Commentary* (Grand Rapids, MI: William B. Eerdmans, 2012), 1007, who states that Christian fellowship is one "invited into this divine intercommitment" of the Father and Son.

99 McGrath, *Christian Theology*, 420. See also Tyron Inbody, *The Faith of the Christian Church: An Introduction to Theology* (Grand Rapids, MI: William B. Eerdmans, 2005), 261, who is of the mind that in spite of the universality of church at a spiritual or faith level, it is grounded in the "spiritual unity of local congregations."

100 Hans Küng, *The Church*, trans. Ray and Rosaleen Ockenden (New York: Sheed & Ward, 1968), 272.

101 See also 1 Cor. 12:4-6; 2 Cor. 1:21-22; Gal. 4:6; Eph. 2:20-22; 2 Thess. 2:13-14; 1 Pet. 1:2.

102 Daniel L. Migliore, *Faith Seeking Understanding: An Introduction to Christian Theology* (Grand Rapids, MI: William B. Eerdmans, 1991), 61-62.

103 Ibid., 63.

104 Ibid., 69.

105 McGrath, *Christian Theology*, 253.

106 Miroslav Volf, *After our Likeness: The Church as the Image of the Trinity* (Grand Rapids, MI: William B. Eerdmans, 1998), 209.

107 McGrath, *Christian Theology*, 254-55. See also Colin E. Gunton, *The One, The Three and The Many: God, Creation and the Culture of Modernity* (The

Bampton Lectures 1992) (Cambridge: Cambridge University Press, 1993), 163, who says that perichoresis is an "implication of the unity-in-variety of the divine economic involvement in the world … [I]n eternity Father, Son and Spirit share a dynamic mutual reciprocity, interpenetration and inter animation."

108 Volf, *After Our Likeness*, 212.

109 Ibid.

110 Ibid. 213.

111 Ibid., 211.

112 Jürgen Moltmann, *The Spirit of Life: A Universal Affirmation*, trans. Margaret Khol (Minneapolis, MN: Fortress Press, 1992), 220.

113 J. N. D. Kelly, *Early Christian Creeds*, 3rd ed. (London: Longman Group Limited, 1972), 6-12, 205-27. The Apostles' Creed is thought to be traced to a creed that developed in Rome around the end of the second century. The origin of this creed is not clear; but its early form is likely preserved in the Interrogatory Creed of Hippolytus's Apostolic Tradition (215 C.E.). The Apostle's Creed includes only the words "holy" and "catholic" while the Nicene uses all four marks of the church. See also Wolfhart Pannenberg, *The Apostles' Creed: In Light of Today's Questions*, trans. Margaret Kohl (London: SCM Press, 1972), 1-2; Gordon H. Clark, *What Do Presbyterians Believe? The Westminster Confession: Yesterday and Today* (Philadelphia: The Presbyterian Reformed Publishing Co., 1965), 1-8; John H. Leith, ed., *Creeds of the Churches: A Reader in Christian Doctrine from the Bible to the Present* (New York: Doubleday & Company Inc., 1963), 22-23.

114 Inbody, *The Faith*, 261.

115 Ibid.

116 Küng, *The Church*, 274.

117 Ibid.

118 Stanley J. Grenz, *Theology for the Community of God* (Grand Rapids, MI: William B. Eerdmans; Vancouver: Regent College Publishing, 2000), 468.

119 Inbody, *The Faith*, 261.

120 *The Book of Order of the Presbyterian Church of Aotearoa New Zealand*, adopted by the General Assembly, September 2006, last amended October 2018.

121 Kupu Whakapono (Confession of Faith) and Commentary, adopted by PCANZ General Assembly, October 2010.

122 Kupu Whakapono, paragraph 3, line 8.

123 Commentary, Kupu Whakapono, 12, paragraph 69.

124 Kupu Whakapono, paragraph 4, line 5.

125 Commentary, Kupu Whakapono, 14, paragraph 91.

126 Kupu Whakapono, paragraph 5, lines 1-5.

127 Commentary, Kupu Whakapono, 17, paragraph 108.

128 Ibid., 17-18, paragraph 109.

129 Ibid., 18, paragraph 113.

130 Ibid., 18, paragraph 114.

131 Ibid., 18, paragraph 113.

132 Ibid., 2, paragraph 1.

133 Ibid., 4, paragraph 91.

134 BOO, 1.3.

135 BOO, 1.5.2.

136 BOO, 1.5.3.

137 BOO, 1.5.4.

138 BOO, 1.6

139 BOO, 14.12.2.

140 BOO, 14.13.1(c), (d).

141 BOO, 11.2.2.

142 BOO, 11.2.5. See chapter 11.3 for the full duties of Te Aka Puaho.

143 BOO, 11.2.3.

144 "Terms of Reference for Council of Asian Congregations," Assembly Reports, E1-29, GA 2000, PCANZ.

145 Ibid.

146 BOO, 13.2.(d).

147 BOO, 13. 4. (d). b.

148 BOO, 8.3.

149 BOO, 8.9.1(a)-(g).

150 BOO, 8.9.1(a).

151 BOO, 8.9.3.

152 Peter Matheson, "The Settler Church 1840-1870," in *Presbyterians in Aotearoa 1840-1990*, ed. Dennis McEldowney, 15-42 (Wellington: Presbyterian Church of New Zealand, 1990), 15. Nearly two-fifths of its ministers and all of its missionaries were reported to have left the church to form the Free Church of Scotland.

153 Ibid., 16.

154 Ibid.

155 John Dickson, *History of the Presbyterian Church of New Zealand* (Dunedin: J. Wilkie & Co., 1899), 17.

156 Matheson, "Settler Church," 21.

157 Ibid.

158 Dickson, *History of the Presbyterian Church*, 19.

159 Matheson, "Settler Church," 30.

160 John R. Elder, *The History of the Presbyterian Church of New Zealand 1840-1940* (Christchurch: Presbyterian Bookroom, 1940). Appendix, Register of Ministers, 407-446. The northern church was characterised by the Presbyterian Church of New Zealand and the southern church by the Free Church of Scotland. In 1901 they merged and became one Church.

161 Ibid.

162 John McKean, *The Church in a Special Colony: A History of the Presbyterian Synod of Otago and Southland 1866-1991* (Dunedin: Synod of Otago and Southland, 1994), 195-200.

163 Horace John Crawford, *A Noble Record: One Hundred Years of Presbyterian Church Government in Auckland 1856-1956* (Auckland: Presbyterian Church of New Zealand, 1956), 33.

164 Ibid., 34.

165 Peter Matheson, *First Church of Otago: The People's Church* (Dunedin: First Church of Otago, 1998), 23.

166 Ibid., 24.

167 Ibid.

168 Ibid.

169 Matheson, "Settler Church," 39. The lack of interest and effort by most European Presbyterians in New Zealand to integrate and work with Māori, according to Matheson, was shameful: "Unlike the Anglicans or Wesleyans there was no real Presbyterian expertise in the field, and their embarrassment is hinted at by their appointment of German Lutherans as their missionaries."

170 J. N Smith, *Upon Them the Light Shined: A Brief History of the Presbyterian Māori Mission* (Auckland: Presbyterian Church of New Zealand, 1952), 9.

171 Laurie Barber, "The Expanding Frontier (1901-1930)," in *Presbyterians in Aotearoa 1840-1990*, ed. Dennis McEldowney, 74-102 (Wellington: Presbyterian Church of New Zealand, 1990), 91.

172 Ibid.

173 Ibid. While Te Kooti's influence in the Urewera is significant and the centre of Ringatu, and because Kēnana saw himself as his successor, Te Kooti moved on from there and was active in other places.

174 Sonny Riini and Diane Gilliam-Knight, "An Historical Perspective Helps," in *He Taonga hei Whakatu Honohono: A Gift Towards Partnership*, Te Hinota Māori, Book 1, 12-15 (Wellington: Presbyterian Church of Aotearoa New Zealand, 1992), 12. They posit that the deaconesses were not seen as

a threat by Māori; rather, they were greatly revered and their works were admired.

175 Lachy Paterson, "The Rise and Fall of Women Field Workers within the Presbyterian Māori Mission, 1907-1970," in *Mana Māori and Christianity*, ed. Hugh Morrison, Lachy Peterson, Brett Knowles and Murray Rae, 179-204 (Wellington: Huia Publishers, 2012), 180.

176 Murray Rae, "The Subversive Theology of Rua Kēnana," in *Mana Māori and Christianity*, ed. Hugh Morrison, Lachy Paterson, Brett Knowles and Murray Rae, 223-242 (Wellington: Huia Publishers, 2012), 233.

177 James Irwin, *From Dependence to Autonomy* (Annual Lecture, Whakatane) (Dunedin: Presbyterian Historical Society, 1984), 10.

178 Ibid.

179 John G. Laughton, *From Forest Trail to City Street: The Story of the Presbyterian Church among the Māori People* (Christchurch: Presbyterian Bookroom, 1961), 49.

180 Riini and Gilliam-Knight, "An Historical Perspective Helps," 13.

181 Māori Synod, Presbyterian Church of New Zealand, *A Māori View of the Hunn Report* (Christchurch: Presbyterian Bookroom, 1961).

182 Barber, "The Expanding Frontier," 91. Māori prophet Rua Kenana of the Ringatu faith made an agreement with John Laughton that he would minister to the older Māori while Laughton could concentrate on the children in schools. See also footnote 243.

183 H. J. Fletcher, *Fletcher of Taupo*, unpublished document, Wanganui, New Zealand, 1975, 45. Henry Fletcher was a European minister commissioned by the Presbyterian Church to serve in the Māori mission field. He was reported on many occasions to have gone to where Māori were gathered, whether in the bush or across Lake Taupo, rather than waiting for them to visit the mission station.

184 Māori Synod, *A Māori View*, 28.

185 Laughton, *From Forest Trail*, 21.

186 Ibid., 22.

187 Raeburn Lange, "Ordained Ministry in Māori Christianity 1853-1900," *JRH* 27, no. 1 (February 2003): 47-66, 47. For further references to the importance of Māori Christians to the spread of Christianity in New Zealand see also Raeburn Lange, *Island Ministers: Indigenous Leadership in Nineteenth Century Pacific Islands Christianity* (Christchurch: Macmillan Brown Centre for Pacific Studies, University of Canterbury, 2005), 150; William Williams, *Christianity among the New Zealanders* (London: n. p., 1867), 155. Cited by Lange, *Island Ministers*, 150; Richard Taylor, *The Past and Present of New Zealand, with its Prospects for the Future* (London: n. p., 1868), 34. Cited by Lange, *Island Ministers*, 152; Rua D. Rakena, *The Māori Response to the Gospel: A Study of*

Māori-Pakeha Relations in the Māori Methodist Missions from its Beginnings to the Present Day (Auckland: Wesley Historical Society, 1971), 15; Alan Ward, *A Show of Justice: Racial "Amalgamation" in Nineteenth Century New Zealand* (Auckland: Auckland University Press, 1995); H. W. Tucker, *Memoir of the Life and Episcopate of George Augustus Selwyn*, vol. 2 (London: Gardner, 1879), 301; Octavius Hadfield, *Māoris of By-gone Days* (Gisborne: Te Rau, 1902), 12-13; S. J. Brittan and G. F., C. W. and A. V. Grace, eds., *A Pioneer Missionary Among the Māoris 1850-1879* (Palmerston North: Bennet, n. d.), 84;

188 Laughton, *From Forest Trail*, 54.

189 Riini and Gilliam-Knight, "An Historical Perspective Helps," 13.

190 Irwin, *From Dependence to Autonomy*, 15.

191 Ibid.

192 Wayne Tekaawa, *Ko te Amorangi ki mua, ko te hapai o ki muri*, Inaugural Lecture, Knox Centre for Ministry and Leadership, Dunedin, (Unpublished paper, 2013), 5-6.

193 Tekaawa, *Ko te Amorangi ki mua*, 8.

194 Ibid,, 7-8.

195 Elder, *History Presbyterian Church*, 336. Elder noted that as early as 1868, the Synod of Otago and Southland resolved to organise a mission among local Chinese miners.

196 Matheson, "Settler Church," 40.

197 "The Missionary to the Chinese in Otago," *The Evangelist* 3, no. 4 (1 April 1871): 124.

198 "Chinese Mission," *The Evangelist* 3, no. 5 (1 June 1871): 188-189. Two months later, it was noted that the number of Chinese gathering for worship in Tuapeka had increased from eighteen to twenty-six. Of this number, seven were members and the rest were regular visitors.

199 "Missionary to the Chinese," *The Evangelist* 4, no. 4 (1 April 1872): 125. "The influence of the Chinese converts in Tuapeka is extending, and serving to strengthen Paul's [Chin] position and influence. They have indicated their desire to help the work also."

200 "The Chinese in Otago," *The Evangelist* 4, no. 5 (1 May 1872): 129-132.

201 Regarding Christian missions in China see Francis M. DuBose, ed., "The Journal of Matthew Ricci," in *Classics of Christian Missions*, 167-172 (Nashville, TN: Broadman Press, 1979), 167; John W. Witek, "Christianity and China: Universal Teaching from the West," in *China and Christianity: Burdened Past, Hopeful Future*, ed. Stephen Uhalley, Jr. and Xiaoxin Wu, 11-28 (New York: M. E. Sharpe, 2000), 17; Nicolas Standaert, ed., *Handbook of Christianity in China, Vol. 1, 635-1800* (Leiden: Brill, 2001a), 311; Nicolas Standaert, "Christianity in Late Ming and Early Qing China as a Case of Cultural Transmission," in *China and Christianity: Burdened Past, Hopeful Future*, ed. Stephen Uhalley, Jr. and

Xiaoxin Wu (New York: M. E. Sharp Inc., 2001b), 81-116, 84; Jesse G. Lutz, "A Profile of Chinese Protestant Evangelists in the Mid-nineteenth Century," in *Authentic Chinese Christianity: Preludes to its Development (Nineteenth and Twentieth Centuries)*, ed. Ku Wei-ying and Koen De Ridder, 67-86 (Leuven: Leuven University Press, 2001), 71. For the effectiveness of Korean Christian converts in Korea see Lak-Geoon George Paik, *The History of Protestant Missions in Korea 1832-1910*, 3rd ed. (Seoul: Yonsei University Press, 1980), 32; J. Ross, "The Christian Dawn in Korea," *The Missionary Review of the World* 3, no. 4 (1890): 242-243; H. G. Underwood, *The Call of Korea* (New York: Leming H. Revell Company, 1908), 137.

202 James Ng, *The Presbyterian Church of New Zealand and the Chinese* (Christchurch: Presbyterian Historical Society, 1987), 5. Ng notes that Cowie was only fluent in the Fukeinese language.

203 Ibid.

204 Alexander Don, "Our Chinese Mission," *The N.Z. Presbyterian* (1 October 1884): 64-65, 64.

205 Alexander Don, "Chinese Mission Work in Otago: Annual Up-Country Tour 1900-01," *The Christian Outlook*, 1901, Dunedin, Hocken Pamphlet collection v.071 no. 24, 1. Don noted that Loie conducted the tours in 1898-99 and 1899-1901.

206 Alexander Don, "Annual Up-Country Tour 1894-95: Among Otago Chinese," *The Christian Outlook*, Dunedin, 1895, Hocken Pamphlet collection v.071 no. 27, 58.

207 Ibid.

208 Ibid.

209 Chinese Presbyterian Church of Dunedin, Annual Report, 1905, noted that although there was a decline in the Chinese population of the city, attendance at the Chinese in Dunedin gradually increased. The 1907 Annual Report noted that average attendance to the afternoon service increased from 39 to 44. In 1909, for a period of 5 months under F. L. Law's leadership, the average attendance jumped to 52, the largest since the church opened in 1897.

210 Susan Irvine, "'Teacher' Don: The Mission to the Chinese in Otago," in *Building God's Own Country: Historical Essays on Religion in New Zealand*, ed. John Stenhouse and Jane Thompson, 155-168 (Dunedin: University of Otago Press, 2004), 163.

211 A. L. Miller, "Minister's Report," Chinese Church of Dunedin Annual Report, 1940. Dunedin: PCANZ Archives.

212 Stuart Vogel, "Principles and Guidelines for Parishes and Presbyteries," a Handbook prepared by the committee on the Development of Asian Ministries within The Presbyterian Church of Aotearoa New Zealand. (Unpublished, 1995), 1.

213 Council of Asian Congregations Report, Assembly Reports, F16-1, PCANZ General Assembly, 2004.

214 Minutes, Session 8.14, General Assembly 1993, PCANZ, 57.

215 Stuart Vogel, "Principles and Guidelines," 4-5.

216 Ibid., 5. It was noted in the report that it was "appropriate to appoint" a church leader of the same ethnic and cultural background as the congregation.

217 Reports, F16-1, General Assembly 2004, PCANZ. There are 22 Korean ministers in the Korean Ministers Association, of which 19 have been trained in the Presbyterian Church of Korea.

218 Correspondence, Stuart Vogel (Secretary Asian Advisory Council) to Tokerau Joseph, 12 June 2012. Of the 33 ministers of Asian descent in PCANZ, only 4 were trained in the PCANZ.

219 Council of Asian Congregations Annual Report, Auckland, 2005. It was noted that some Asian congregations found it difficult to communicate with and understand certain aspects of the work of the National Office of the PCANZ. Of particular concern for Asian congregations was the matter of national and presbytery levies.

220 Stuart Vogel, "Inklings of an Altered State: Counter-imaging the Presbyterian Church of Aotearoa-New Zealand within a Culturally Diverse Society," Discussion Paper 1 (unpublished paper) presented to PCANZ General Assembly, 2012, 7.

221 Ibid.

222 Ibid., 8.

223 Jim Bernard Chambers, *A Peculiar People: Congregationalism in New Zealand 1840-1984, Including The Congregational Union of New Zealand 1884-1984* (Levin: Congregational Union of New Zealand, 1984), 125. As early as the 1920s missionaries in the Pacific were urged to notify the Congregational Union of New Zealand when members of their churches were visiting New Zealand so hospitality could be offered.

224 Robert L. Challis, *Social Problems of Non-Māori Polynesians in New Zealand*, Technical Paper No. 41, presented at the South Pacific Commission, Sydney, 1953, 3. Challis was a missionary and minister of the Congregational Church who served in both the Pacific and New Zealand. See also previous chapter on early Christian missions in the Pacific.

225 *Proceedings of the General Assembly 1969*, Presbyterian Church of New Zealand, 1969, 160-161.

226 Ibid., 160-61. It had a Management Board that dealt with policy matters and was responsible for the support of the ministry and calling ministers, in consultation with the churches concerned. As a result of recognising and receiving the Pacific Islanders' Church (PIC) as an integral component of the

Congregational Union, it was agreed by the PCANZ to give the Management
Board the status of an Assembly Standing Committee.

227 Ibid., 34-36. The Cook Islanders were apparently the first group at the
Beresford Street church, as early as 1942, followed by Niueans in 1947.

228 Ibid., 36.

229 Robert L. Challis, "Pacific Islanders in New Zealand," in *Bulletin for Schools*
(Wellington: Schools Publication Branch, Department of Education, 1970), 72.

230 Ibid., 73.

231 Uili Feleterika Nolise, "A History of the Pacific Islanders' Congregational
Church in New Zealand 1943 – 1969," M.Th. thesis, University of Otago, 1978,
148. The apparent numerical majority early on in the life of the Auckland
church owing, perhaps, to their New Zealand citizenship that enabled them
to enter and stay in New Zealand much easier. But, the lenient Government
immigration policy during the 1950s and 1960s encouraged consistent annual
migration from Samoa that saw the Samoan membership of the church
supersede that of Cook Islanders and Niueans.

232 Ibid.

233 Ibid., 134.

234 Betty K. Duncan, "Christianity: Pacific Island Traditions," in *Religions of
New Zealanders*, ed. P. Donovan, 128-141 (Palmerston North: Dunmore Press,
1990), 129.

235 Nokise, "History of the PIC," 113.

236 Ibid., 11. See also *Proceedings of the General Assembly 1969*, Presbyterian
Church of New Zealand, 160.

237 See John Barker, "An Outpost in Papua: Anglican Missionaries and
Melanesian Teachers among the Maisin, 1902-1934," in *Studies in Christian
Mission*, ed. Marc R. Spindler, 79-106 (Leiden: Brill Academic Publishers,
2005), 81; William Wyatt Gill, *From Darkness to Light in Polynesia* (London:
London Missionary Society, 1894), 364; Maretu, *Cannibals and Converts:
Radical Change in the Cook Islands*, trans. and ed. Marjorie T. Crocombe, 101-
53 (Suva, Fiji: Institute of Pacific Studies, USP, 1983); Peggy Brock, "Setting
the Record Straight: New Christians and Mission Christianity," in *Studies in
Christian Missions*, ed. Marc R. Spindler, 107-128 (Leiden: Brill Academic
Publishers, 2005), 113; John Williams, *A Narrative of Missionary Enterprises
in the South Sea Islands* (London: John Snow, 1842), 77; Kon-Tiki Makani,
"Ekalesia Niue: An Indigenous Church in the Making," M.Th. thesis, Pacific
Theological College, 1993, 6; Raeburn Lange, *The Origins of the Christian
Ministry in the Cook Islands and Samoa*, MacMillan Brown Working Paper
Series, no. 6 (Christchurch: MacMillan Brown Center for Pacific Studies,
University of Canterbury, 1997), 6; Lalomilo Kamo, *The Samoan Culture and
the Christian Gospel* (Suva, Fiji: USP, 1996), 82; Richard Lovett, *The History
of the London Missionary Society, 1795-1895*, Vol. 2 (London: Frowd, 1899),

Appendix ii, 747. See also R. Pierce Beaver, "The History of Mission Strategy," in *Perspectives on the World Christian Movement*, ed. Ralph D. Winter and Steven C. Hawthorne, 3rd ed., 241-252 (Pasadena, CA: William Carey Library, 1981), 248, who says that, according to Rufus Anderson, new churches were to be put under their own pastors and were to develop their own local and regional polity.

238 Nokise, *History of the PIC*, 148.

239 Ibid.

240 *Year Book 2009* (Wellington: PCANZ, 2009). See p. 41 for Manukau PIC (Samoan) and p. 111 for Invercargill PIC (Samoan).

241 Ibid. See p. 34 for Samoan Presbyterian Church Onehunga, p. 41 for Manukau Cook Islanders' Presbyterian Church, p. 74 for Cook Islands Presbyterian Church (Wellington Region), and p. 112 for Invercargill Cook Islanders' Presbyterian Church.

242 Ibid. See p. 29 for Avondale Union Parish (Samoan Speaking Fellowship, and p. 73 for St. James' Presbyterian (Niuean) and St. James' Presbyterian (English).

243 Jehu J. Hanciles, "Migration and Mission: he Religious Significance of the North-South Divide," in *Mission in the 21st Century: Exploring the Five Marks of Global Mission*, ed. Andrew Walls and Cathy Ross, 118-129 (London: Darton, Longman and Todd, 2008), 118.

244 Gerald A. Arbuckle, SM, *Earthing the Gospel: An Inculturation Handbook for Pastoral Workers* (London: Geoffrey Chapman, 1990), 17.

245 Daniel W. Hardy, "The Future of Theology in a Complex World," in *Christ and Context: The Confrontation between Gospel and Culture*, ed. Hilary D. Regan and Alan J. Torrance, 21-42 (Edinburgh: T&T Clark, 1993), 22-23.

246 Lesslie Newbigin, *The Gospel in a Pluralistic Society* (Grand Rapids, MI: William B. Eerdmans, 1989), 154.

247 Ibid., 190.

248 Anne Keary, "Colonial Constructs and Cross-Cultural Interaction: Comparing Missionary/Indigenous Encounters in Northwestern America and Eastern Australia," in *Beyond Conversion and Syncretism: Indigenous Encounters with Missionary Christianity, 1800-2000*, ed. David Lindenfeld and Miles Richardson, 243-298 (Oxford: Berghahn Books, 2012), 284.

249 Graham Ward, *Cultural Transformation and Religious Practice* (Cambridge: Cambridge University Press, 2005), 114.

250 Andrew F. Walls, *The Missionary Movement in Christian History: Studies in the Transmission of Faith* (Maryknoll, NY: Orbis Books, 1996), 24.

251 Eric H. F, Law, *The Bush Was Blazing But Not Consumed: Developing a Multicultural Community through Dialogue and Liturgy* (St. Louis, MO: Chalice Press, 1996), 43.

252 Ibid.

Endnotes

253 Stuart Vogel, *Inklings of an Altered State: Counter-imaging the Presbyterian Church of Aotearoa New Zealand*, Discussion Paper 1 (unpublished paper), presented to General Assembly of the PCANZ, 2012, 6-7.

254 Kevin Ward, *Cultural Diversity and Unity in Christ: The Presbyterian Church of Aotearoa New Zealand in a Land of Many Cultures*, unpublished paper, Knox Centre for Ministry and Leadership, Dunedin, New Zealand, 2013, 6.

255 Details from 87 congregations (response rate 55%), 49 parishioner questionnaires (response rate 21%) and 17 parishioner interviews, 33 minister questionnaires (response rate 41%) and 22 interviews.

256 Emerson and Kim, *Multiracial Congregations*, 217. See also Emerson, *People of the Dream*, 35.

257 Emerson, *People of the Dream*, 35.

258 Ibid.

259 Population figures were taken from the Census 2006

260 Korie L. Edwards, "Bring Race to the Center: The Importance of Race in Racially Diverse Religious Organizations," *JSSR* 47, no. 1 (2008): 5-9.

261 Ibid., 6.

262 97% in European congregations, 98% in Māori congregations, 100% in Asian congregations, 76% in Pacific Islander congregations.

263 64% European, 29% Pacific Islander, 4% Asian, 3% Māori.

264 Kathleen Garces-Foley, "Comparing Catholic and Evangelical Integration Efforts," *JSSR* 47, no. 1 (2008): 17-22, 21. See also Gerardo Marti, *Mosaic*, 156.

265 Edwards, "Bring Race to the Center," 6.

266 Pacific Islander ministers 17%, Māori 7%, Asian 3%

267 67% of minister sample were European, 27% were Pacific Islander, 6% were Asian.

268 91% of the sample joined predominantly European congregations. This number consisted of all Europeans in the sample and 75% of Pacific Islanders.

269 Craig R. Prentiss, ed., *Religion and the Creation of Race and Ethnicity: An Introduction* (New York: New York University Press, 2003), 1-2.

270 World Council of Churches, *Christian Perspectives on Theological Anthropology: A Faith and Order Study Document* (Faith and Order Paper 199 (Geneva: World Council of Churches, 2005), 7.

271 David. E. Stevens, *God's New Humanity: A Biblical Theology of Multiethnicity for the Church* (Eugene, Oregon: Wipf & Stock, 2012), 175.

272 Anthony J. Gittins, "The Universal in the Local: Power, Piety and Paradox in the Formation of Missionary Community," in *Mission and Culture: The Louis J. Luzbetak Lectures*, The American Society of Missiology Series, ed. Stephen B. Bevans, 133-87 (Maryknoll, NY: Orbis, 2012), 164.

273 Stevens, *God's New Humanity*, 117.

274 Marcus J. Borg and John Dominic Crossman, *The First Paul: Reclaiming the Radical Visionary behind the Church's Conservative Icon* (New York: HarperOne, 2009), 186.

275 Ibid., 253. Stevens' argues that the "building materials" used to construct the walls that divide Christian communities include sociological dynamics of individualism, consumerism, choice, and competition, all of which contribute to a greater degree of ethnic homogeneity within local churches and consequent segregation among local churches. In essence, such materials highlight an ethnocentric Christian identity.

276 Eric Law, *The Bush Was Blazing*, 69.

277 Jason A. Goroncy, "Social Identity, Ethnicity, and the Gospel of Reconciliation," unpublished lecture/paper, Knox Centre for Ministry and Leadership, Dunedin, New Zealand, 2012.

278 Stuart Vogel, "The Self-understanding of a Multi-Ethnic Church," Discussion Paper Two, presented to the General Assembly of the PCANZ, 2012. Here Vogel argues that "the primary calling and aim of the Christian community is to 'worship God and enjoy him forever'. It is not to be a multi-cultural or even to witness our oneness in Christ."

279 Philip Culbertson, ed., *Counselling Issues and South Pacific Communities* (Auckland: Accent Publications, 1997), 15.

280 Richard W. Brislin, Kenneth Cushner, Craig Cherrie and Mahealani Yong, *Intercultural Interactions: A Practical Guide*, Vol. 9, Cross-Cultural Research and Methodology Series (Beverly Hills, CA: Sage, 1986). In brief, they posit that "people typically have difficulties when moving across cultures. Suddenly, and with little warning, behaviours and attitudes that proved necessary for obtaining goals in their own culture are no longer useful. Further, familiar behaviors that marked a well-adjusted person in their own culture are seen as indicative of an ill-mannered person."

281 Dietrich Bonhoeffer, *Life Together*, trans. from the 5th edition by John W. Doberstein (London: SCM Press, 1954), 16.

282 Ibid., 16-17.

283 Ibid.

284 Ibid., 18.

285 Ibid., 21.

286 The term *interpathy* was first coined by the cross-cultural theologian and pastoral counsellor David Augsburger, in *Pastoral Counseling Across Cultures* (Louisville KY: Westminster John Knox Press, 1986). See also his *Conflict Mediation Across Cultures: Pathways and Patterns* (Louisville, KY: Westminster John Knox Press, 1995).

287 Aart M. van Beek, *Cross-Cultural Counseling*, Creative Pastoral Care and Counseling Series (Minneapolis, MN: Fortress Press, 1996), 76.

Endnotes

288 Eric H. F. Law, *The Wolf Shall Dwell with the Lamb: Spirituality for Leadership in a Multicultural Community* (St. Louis, MO: Chalice Press, 1993), 80.

289 van Beek, *Cross-Cultural Counseling*, 76.

290 Angela Singer, "Welcome Home: Church Considers Cultural Change for Asian Members," SPANZ 54, (Winter 2013): 4-5, 4.

291 Aaron Kuecker, *The Spirit And The "Other": Social Identity, Ethnicity and Intergroup Reconciliation in Luke-Acts* (New York: T&T Clark, 2011), 179.

292 Kathleen Garces-Foley, *Crossing the Ethnic Divide*, 155-158.

293 Law, *The Bush was Blazing*, 83.

294 Eric H. F. Law, *Sacred Acts, Holy Change: Faithful Diversity and Practical Transformation* (St. Louis, Missouri: Chalice Press, 2002), 74.

295 A definition of grace is the favour of God upon human beings (OT) or unmerited divine favour (NT). For an Old Testament definition, see John S. Kselman, "Grace," in *The Anchor Bible Dictionary*, Vol. 2, ed. David Noel Freedman, 1084-1086 (New York: Doubleday, 1992), 1085. For a New Testament definition see Gary S. Shogren, "Grace," in *The Anchor Bible Dictionary*, Vol. 2, ed. David Noel Freedman, 1086-1088 (New York: Doubleday, 1992), 1086.

296 Joseph H. Hellerman, *Jesus and the People Of God: Reconfiguring Ethnic Identity* (Sheffield: Sheffield Phoenix Press, 2007), 202.

297 Bonhoeffer, *Life Together*, 26.

298 McGrath, *Christian Theology*, 434-439.

299 Sinclair B. Ferguson and David F. Wright, eds., *New Dictionary of Theology* (Leicester: InterVarsity Press, 1988), 280.

300 Migliore, *Faith Seeking Understanding*, 220.

301 Ibid., 225.

302 Ibid.

303 Warren Carter, "Matthew's People," in *Christian Origins: A People's History of Christianity*, ed. Richard A. Horsley, 138-161 (Minneapolis, MN: Fortress Press, 2005), 139. He proposes that Matthew's community may have appeared in Antioch as early as 30-40 C.E.

304 Wayne A. Meeks and Robert L. Wilken, *Jews and Christians in Antioch: In the First Four Centuries of the Common Era*, Society of Biblical Literature, Sources for Biblical Study 13 (Missoula, MT: Scholars Press, 1978), 18. See also John P. Meier, "Antioch," in *Antioch and Rome: New Testament Cradles of Catholic Christianity*, ed. Raymond E. Brown and John P. Meier (New York: Paulist Press, 1983), 11-86, 40, who argues the allowing the "kosher" practices of Jewish Christians probably meant that "their meals (and therefore probably Eucharists) would possibly have been held separately."

305 David C. Sim, *The Gospel of Matthew and Christian Judaism: The History and Social Setting of the Matthean Community* (Edinburgh: T. & T. Clark, 1998), 103. "If Gentiles were to remain in the Christian movement, then they must be willing to undergo circumcision (if male) and obey the stipulations of the Jewish law. Anything less than total conversion to (Christian) Judaism would see them exempt themselves from full participation in the Antiochene church."

306 Migliore, *Faith Seeking Understanding*, 226.

307 Moltmann, *The Church*, 243.

308 Zizioulas, *Being as Communion*, 149.

309 Moltmann, *The Church*, 244-45.

310 Ibid., 246.

311 Ibid., 256-57.

312 Ibid., 257-58.

313 Donald A. McGavran, *The Bridges of God: A Study in the Strategy of Missions* (London: World Dominion Press, 1957), 32. Here McGavran argues for effective evangelism and church growth through 'Christward movements' within particular people groups.

314 Walter Kasper, "That They May All Be One," in *Christian Doctrine: A Reader*, ed. Lindsay Hall, Murray Rae and Steve Holmes, 384-85 (London: SCM Press, 2010), 384.

315 Duane Elmer, *Cross-cultural Conflict: Building Relationships for Effective Ministry* (Downers Grove, IL: InterVarsity Press, 1993), 12.

www.ingramcontent.com/pod-product-compliance
Lightning Source LLC
Chambersburg PA
CBHW060226030426

42335CB00014B/1347